PERFECT PAPER PLANES

AMAZING PAPER AIRPLANES THAT REALLY FLY!

Thang Yang

Winner Great International Paper Airplane Contest

Plus Bonus Section!

Mini Paper Planes:

Small but Extraordinary Paper Planes You can Make!

by Michael Weinstein

Mud Puddle Books

NEW YORK

Perfect Paper Planes
Written by Thay Yang

ISBN: 978-1-60311-096-9

This edition published by
Mud Puddle Books, Inc.
54 W. 21st Street
Suite 601
New York, NY 10010
info@mudpuddlebooks.com

Copyright © 1992 by Thay Yang

Originally published by Cypress House
Used by arrangement with Cypress House

Mini Paper Planes:
Small but Extraordinary Paper Planes You Can Make!
Written by Michael Weinstein

Copyright © 2004 by Michael Weinstein

This book was originally published in 2004 as
Stationery Flight:
Extraordinary Paper Planes

Originally published by Cypress House
Used by arrangement with Cypress House

Interior design and layout by Mulberry Tree Press, Inc.

Printed in China

Special thanks to

Say Yang and Vun Yang

A Note from the Author

It gives me great pleasure to offer you these fourteen marvelous aircraft for folding and flying. For some time I've dreamed of sharing the Asian art of paper folding as applied to both simple and sophisticated airplanes as a way of demonstrating the magical uses of paper.

Paper that is neither written on nor read from can still educate and entertain you. In the hands of a clever student, the folding and flying of exotic paper airplanes can teach you about aeronautic principles while inspiring your creative imagination to soar.

Contents

THE PLANES

BONUS SECTION
MINI PAPER PLANES

THE PLANES

Introduction

Beginning with the Wright Brothers' first flight, airplanes have revolutionized the world. Planes of different types with very different purposes began appearing in and being tested by nations around the globe. Planes such as the U.S. F-14 Tomcat, the F-18 Hornet, Stealth fighters and other military planes are high performance descendants of the early dreams of flight.

The industrialized nations of the world have a variety of defensive aircraft, including both fighters and bombers, with individualized style and appearance. All have made a significant impact on world power. Many youngsters dream about flying such aircraft, and, if they are industrious and study hard, they may someday realize their dream.

Right now, young and old alike can learn a great deal about aeronautics while enjoying the challenge of creating modern fighting aircraft through the secret of folding paper airplanes. Never before have such compact and perfect paper airplanes been made. With only one sheet of paper, without knife or scissors, you will be able to create actual replicas of the world's fastest and most powerful planes. If you have ever dreamed of folding exotic paper airplanes, your dream is about to come true.

Once you have mastered the steps that are fully covered in the first two chapters (the Concord and the Jet), creating the rest of the planes should be easy.

In this book, you will find clear diagrams and easy-to-follow instructions to fold these marvelous planes with a single sheet of paper. No cutting is required. No previous book has ever offered techniques for constructing paper aircraft which did not involve cutting (although I offer optional cutting techniques) or the use of more than one piece of paper. No previous book offers this much realism in appearance as well as flight.

I urge you to fold each plane in sequence. You will need to learn the simple folding techniques in the first planes to master the more complex planes at the book's end.

While I hope that you will have fun with the book, you can also learn from it. After you have folded these planes several times, I think you'll want to experiment: change the shape, combine different techniques, learn to create other airplanes. That's what happened to me. If you are patient and let your creativity and imagination soar, it will happen to you as well.

Glossary

Aileron (or flap) ▪ the hinged, movable trailing edge of a wing used to alter wing shape (camber), and therefore lift and drag, especially during landing.

Crease ▪ the result of a fold

Elevator ▪ a horizontal control surface at the trailing edge of the plane that can be bent up or down to control or cause climbing or diving.

Fin ▪ the upright part of the tail.

Fuselage ▪ the body of the airplane.

Rudder ▪ a vertical control surface at the trailing edge of the plane that can be moved to initiate a right or left turn.

Stabilizer ▪ the fixed horizontal part at the tail of the plane.

Trim ▪ fold or bend to control turning, climbing or diving.

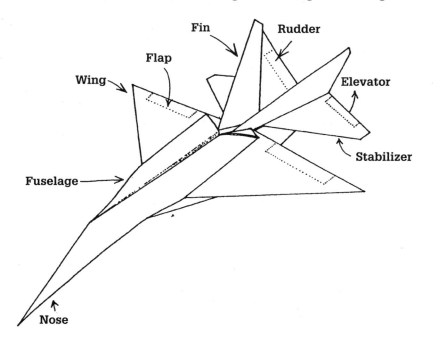

Flying Tips for Paper Airplanes

1) Fold paper evenly. A firm sturdy shape flies best.

2) Fold the tail fin straight up.

3) Use pressure when folding to ensure crisp points.

4) Throw straight.

5) If plane loops, add weight (e.g., a paperclip) to the nose.

6) To climb, trim the elevators up. To dive, trim the elevators down.

7) Trim rudders to the right for right turns and to the left for left turns.

8) For stunts, trim one aileron down and the other up. This will make the plane spin and roll as it flies.

Guide to Symbols

Indication of a hidden fold

Fold line — — — — — — — — — — — —

Crease line ....

Distance }

Inches = "

Fold direction ——→

Fold back & forth (or side to side)

Fold behind

Fold then unfold

Turn model over

Unfold

Where to press your thumb & index finger

Practice Fold #1:
Inside-Reverse Fold

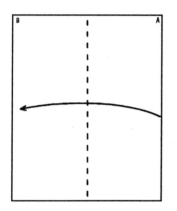

1) Fold the paper in half.

2) Fold the bottom half diagonally to the left side.

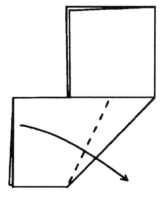

3) Fold diagonally back down.

4) Unfold completely

5) This is what the paper should look like with crease lines.

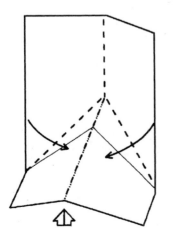

6) Fold the two sides together and raise up the center fold.

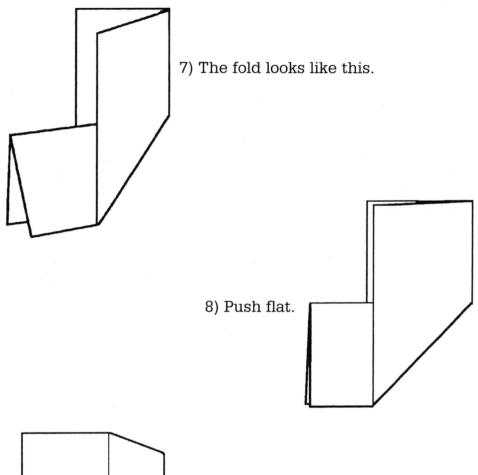

7) The fold looks like this.

8) Push flat.

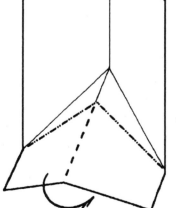

9) Open the paper half way and fold inward on the marked crease lines.

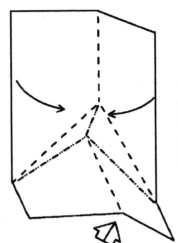

10) Fold the two sides of the paper together again with the bottom part of the paper folding away to the back side.

11) Close the paper tightly together.

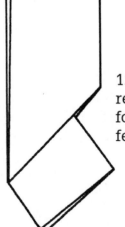

12) Completion of inside-reverse fold. This is a vital folding technique, so try it a few times before moving on.

Practice Fold #2:
The Fuselage Fold

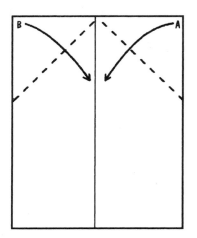

1) Begin with a center line.
Fold corners A and B down to
the center crease line.

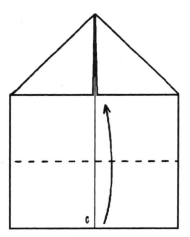

2) Fold C up to meet with
the horizontal bottom
edge of A and B.

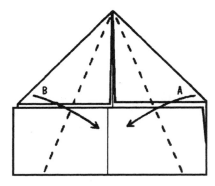

3) Fold A & B to the
center line.

17

4) The coordinates for this fold are 2" down and ½" at the pivot point indicated by the small arrow). Fold side A.

5) unfold.

6) Fold side B.

7) Unfold

8) This diagram shows the two
resulting crease lines crossing.

9) Make an inside-reverse fold
using the existing creases. The
mountain crease rises up between
the two outside edges.

NOTE: This is the fuselage reverse fold.
The fuselage folds for the planes in this
book have similar diagrams but different
coordinates.

10) Proceed through the fold.

11) Flatten loosely.

12) Fuselage fold completed.

13) The tail fin of the plane. Here the inside-reverse fold is going up.

14) To make this reversal, hold the nose end of the plane with your left hand. Place your index finger in the center crease line as shown here. Hold the plane tightly at the nose end, and control the size of the tail fin by sliding your index finger up or down the center crease line. At the lowest point of the belly, reverse it straight up the center with your right hand.

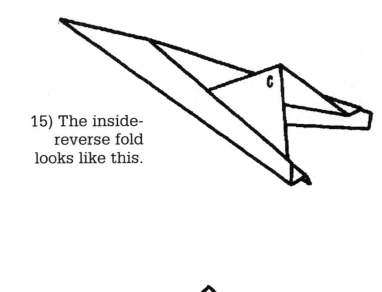

15) The inside-
reverse fold
looks like this.

16) Completed tail fin fold.

Practice these important folds a few times until you are confident. Now you're ready to start folding real planes. You've earned your wings!

CONCORD SST

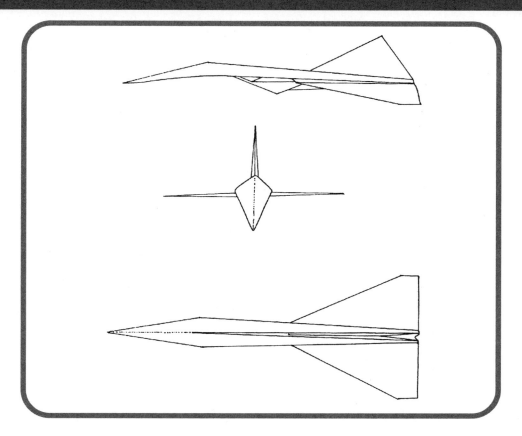

This plane is the simplest to fold of all the planes in this book. It uses basic folding techniques employed throughout the rest of the book. To be successful, follow the steps carefully and precisely. The most important element is to pull up the nose of the plane, and carefully press and align the back, as shown in the drawings. Also, make sure both sides are folded evenly on every fold throughout the plane assembly. Mastering the steps displayed in drawings 16 through 22 in the Concord will greatly improve your future foldings.

NOTE: I suggest that you fold this plane at least five times before going on to other planes.

1

Lay an ordinary piece of 8½" x 11" paper on a flat surface.

2

Fold the paper in half.

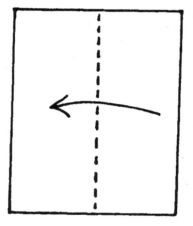

3

Your fold should look like this. Make sure it's folded evenly.

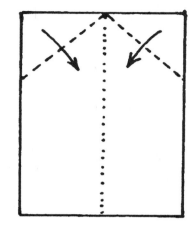

4

Now, unfold the paper and fold down the top corners as indicated by the arrows.

5

Your fold should look like this.

6

Fold the two edges, F & G, toward the centerline, as indicated.

7

It should now look like this.

8

Now, fold the two sides,
B & C, in toward the centerline.

9

After folding toward the
centerline, the paper
should look like this.

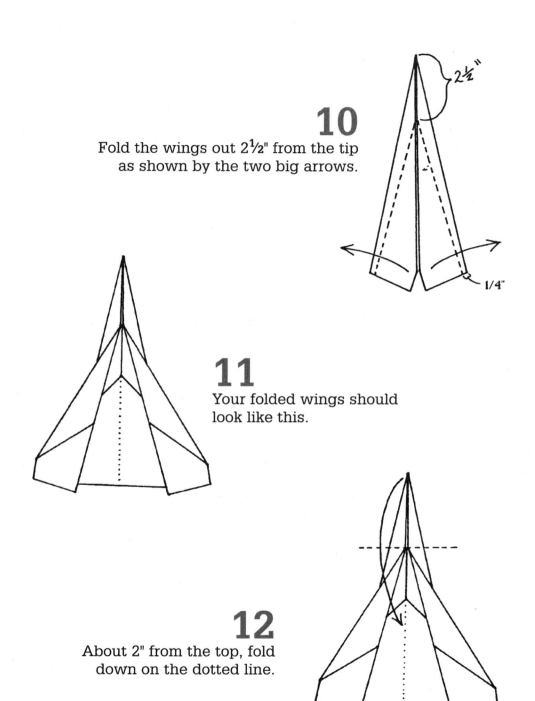

10
Fold the wings out 2½" from the tip
as shown by the two big arrows.

2½"

1/4"

11
Your folded wings should
look like this.

12
About 2" from the top, fold
down on the dotted line.

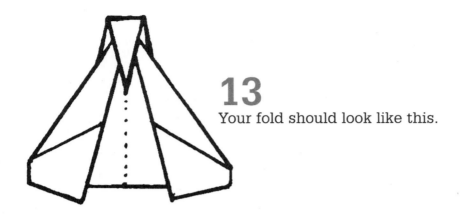

13

Your fold should look like this.

14

After you have folded the nose down, fold the two sides of the plane toward the back as indicated, along the centerline.

side view

15

It should look like this from the side. Pull up the nose as shown by the arrows.

16

After you have pulled up the nose of the plane, position your hands as indicated here.

17

Now, place the plane upside down on a flat surface.

18

Place both of your hands exactly as shown here and hold the plane tightly. Fold back and forth on the dotted line three times on each side.

19

Fold it to the right as shown here, and then to the left.

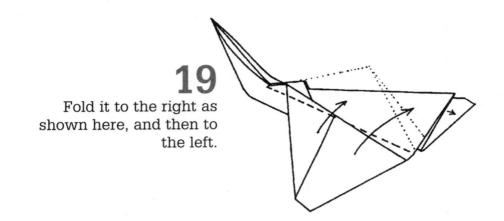

20

Fold it to the left as shown, then to the right. This sets the back into position.

NOTE: Steps 17 to 20 here should be used for all planes in this book.

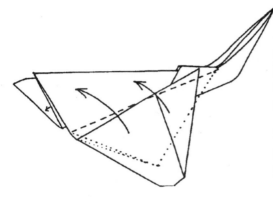

21

Now, flip the plane upright again and press the back down and together as indicated by the arrows.

22

Now, carefully line up the back of the plane by sliding your left hand back and forth as shown here. Then fold the wings up on the dotted line.

23

Your folded wings should look like this.

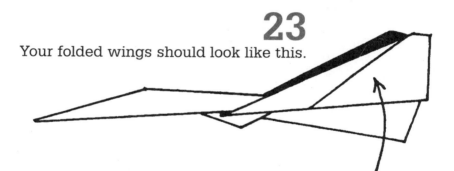

24

To make a tail fin, fold the tail back and forth three or four times at the dotted line.

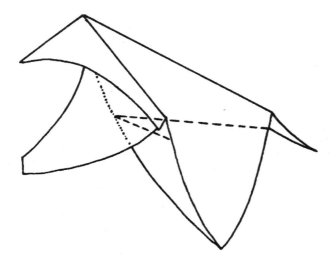

25

After folding the tail back and forth a few times, it should look like this from the rear.

26

Now, carefully lift the tail (fin upward) on the dotted line as indicated here from the rear view.

NOTE: Once you know how to pull up the tail fin, you won't need to fold it back and forth first.

27
Finished version!

CONCORD SST

JET

The Jet is the second primary plane that you must know how to fold before going on to other planes. Carefully follow all the steps and diagrams. Remember, always make sure that all folds are even. Use the techniques you learned from the Concord to help you align the back.

NOTE: I suggest that you fold this plane at least five times before going on to other planes.

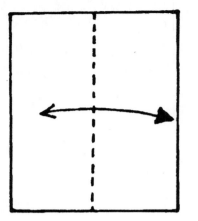

1

Fold paper in half,
then unfold.

2

Fold diagonally at dotted
lines, then unfold.

3

Now, use both hands and
fold the paper up and in
toward the middle.

4

This is how the paper should look. Gently press down from the top.

5

Now, it should look like this.

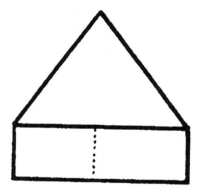

6

Slide your right hand under Flap X as shown here.

7

Flip Flap X over
and onto Flap A.

8

Flap X should line up evenly with
Flap A on the left side.

9

Now, fold Flap X on the
dotted line toward the
centerline.

10

This is how your fold should look.

11

After you have folded Flap X toward the middle flap, flip it to the right side. Notice the B Edge.

12

Now, repeat Steps 9–11 for the left side, and open the flaps to look like this.

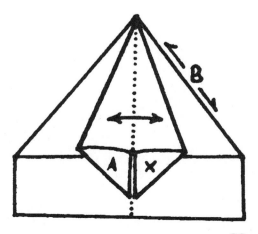

13

Now, flip Flap X to the left,
over Flap A again.

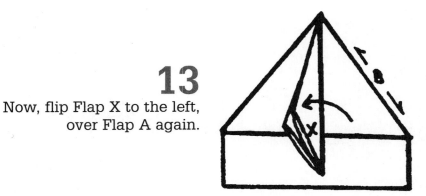

14

Then fold Side B on the dotted
line to the centerline.

15

Now it should
look like this.

16

Now, flip both Flaps A & X to the right side. Repeat Step 14 for the left side.

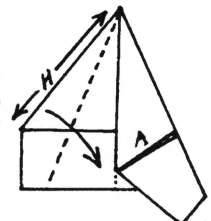

17

Spread Flaps A & X apart like this.

18

Now, flip Flap X to the left side. Then fold Edge B on the dotted line and match it evenly with Edge Z.

19

This is how the fold should look.

20

Now, flip Flaps A & X to the right.

21

Repeat Step 18 on the left side.

22

Then spread the flaps as shown here.

23

Now, you're going to carefully fold the wings out. Fold Flap X to the left side on the dotted line.

2¼"

¼"

x

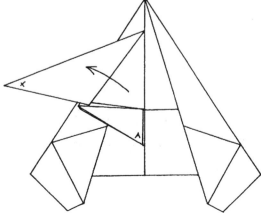

x

24

Your folded wing should look like this.

25

Now, flip Flap X to the right side.

26

Also flip Flap A to the right. Fold Flap A so it matches up evenly with Flap X on the right side.

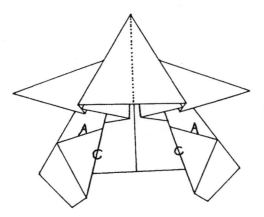

27

Now, move Flap A back to the left so it looks like this. Label A's and C's if you wish.

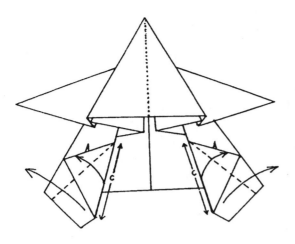

28

Now you're going to fold the stabilizers. Fold Edge C evenly toward Line A.

29

Make sure your folds are even.

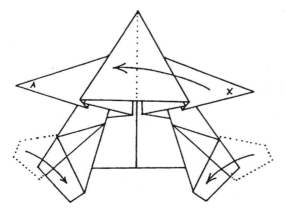

30

Now, unfold the stabilizers and flip Wing X to the left side.

31
Flip Edge B to
the middle.

32
You should have three
crease lines as shown here.

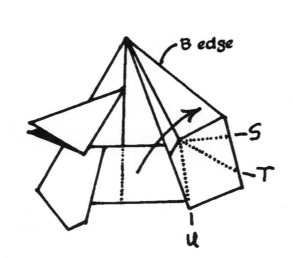

33
Unfold the B Edge further
and you should see the
crease lines—S, T & U.

34

Put your index finger on the middle of Line T and push it outward while pushing Lines S & U inward as indicated by the arrows.

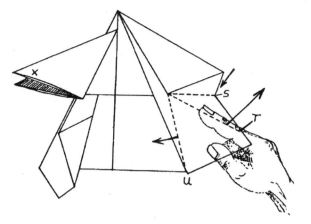

35

Your plane should look like this after you push out Line T. Press down on Point A. Repeat Steps 32–35 on the left side.

36

Open Side A to the left side so the plane looks like this.

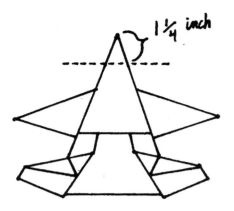

1¼ inch

37

Measure about 1¼ inches from the end of the nose. Fold down the nose along the dotted line.

38

Your fold should look like this.

39

After folding down the nose, fold both sides of the plane's body toward the back as shown.

40

From the side, your plane should look like this. Now, hold the body with your left hand, and, with the other, pull up the nose. Then, as you did on the Concord (Steps 17–20), lay the plane, upside down, on a flat surface and fold the under fuselage back and forth. (This method is used on all the planes in this book.) Notice the 2-inch depth.

2"

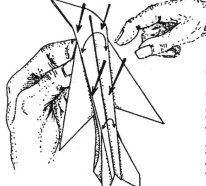

41

Continue to grip the plane firmly in your left hand while using the thumb and index finger of your right hand to press hard along the plane's body, as shown here.

Press hard together

42

Move your right hand under the wings.

43

Carefully apply pressure while sliding your left hand along the back of the plane.

44

After you have completed the back, fold up the wings in the front and back as shown.

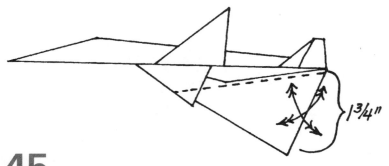

$1\frac{3}{4}''$

45

Fold along the dotted line four times from side to side.

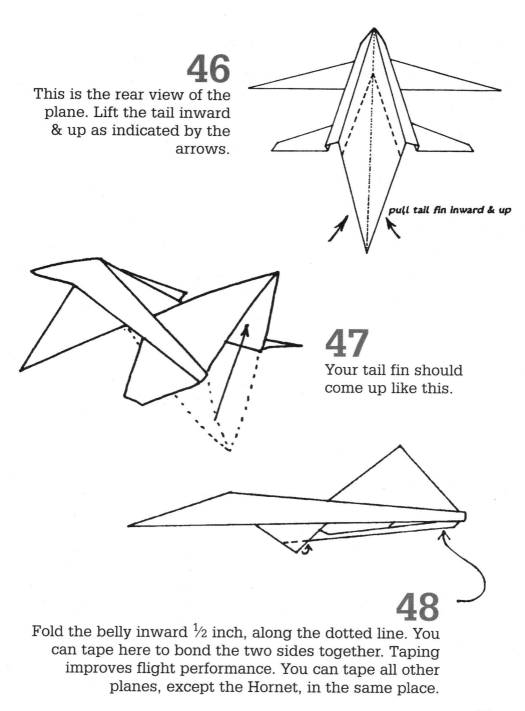

46

This is the rear view of the plane. Lift the tail inward & up as indicated by the arrows.

pull tail fin inward & up

47

Your tail fin should come up like this.

48

Fold the belly inward ½ inch, along the dotted line. You can tape here to bond the two sides together. Taping improves flight performance. You can tape all other planes, except the Hornet, in the same place.

49

The finished version
of the Jet.

50

A   B

Curve the side of the nose for a nice, round,
clean, front end like the one in Diagram B.

51

cut under this fold

cut away

You are now finished with
the Jet, a highly original
plane. If you want the tail to
look more realistic, pull it
down the way it was before
you raised it, then cut along
the dotted lines and push it
up again. Make sure that
it's even with the body.

NOTE: This tail-cut technique may
also be used on the MIG-27.

fold inward

52
Bring the tail up like this.

53
The new tail of the Jet.

SPACE SHUTTLE

In making the Shuttle, the first few folds are exactly the same as the Jet's.

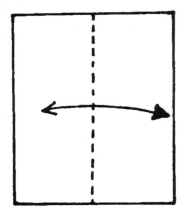

1

Fold paper in half,
then unfold.

2

Fold diagonally at
dotted lines, then
unfold.

3

Now, use both hands and
fold the paper up and in
toward the middle.

4

This is how the
paper should look.
Gently press down
from the top.

5

Now, it should
look like this.

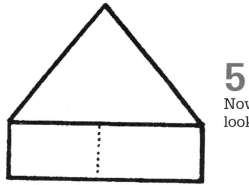

6

Slide your right hand under
Flap X as shown here.

7

Flip Flap X over
and onto Flap A.

8

Flap X should line up
evenly with Flap A on
the left side.

9

Now, fold Flap X on the
dotted line toward the
centerline.

10

This is how your fold should look.

11

After you have folded Flap X toward the middle flap, flip it to the right side. Notice the B Edge.

12

Now, repeat Steps 9–11 for the left side, and open the flaps to look like this.

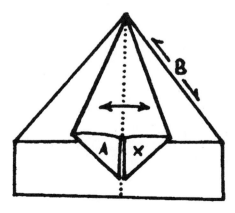

13

Now, flip Flap X to the left, over Flap A again.

14

Then fold Side B on the dotted line to the centerline.

15

Now it should look like this.

16

Now, flip both Flaps A & X
to the right side. Repeat
Step 14 for the left side.

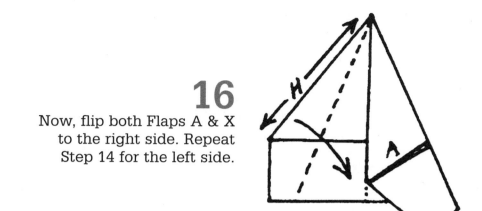

17

Spread Flaps A & X
apart like this.

18

Now, flip Flap X to the left side. Then
fold Edge B on the dotted line and
match it evenly with Edge Z.

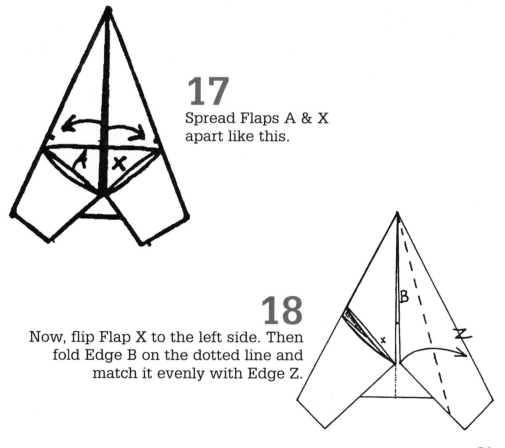

19

This is how the fold
should look.

20

Now, flip Flaps A & X
to the right.

21

Repeat Step 18
on the left side.

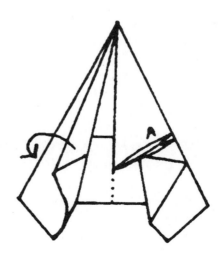

22

Then spread the flaps as shown here.

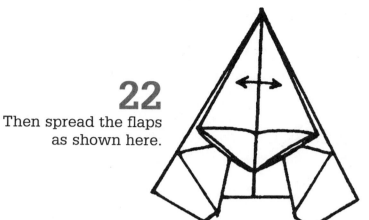

23

This is how your paper should look after completing Steps 1–22 In the Jet chapter. Now fold Flap X to the left as the arrow indicates.

24

Fold the right wing out to the right along the dotted line.

2"

3/8"

25

Your right wing fold should look like this. Now make the same fold on the left side.

26

Now, fully open Flap X to the left and fold along the dotted line so that Corner X is on Corner H.

27

This is how your fold should look. Do the same on the other side.

28

Separate your newly folded flaps. This is the front stabilizer. Fold the nose along the dotted line.

29

This is how the fold should look. Now fold both sides of the plane away from you.

30

The plane should look like this. Next, turn the plane over and pinch the belly about 1⅓" into the fuselage (along the dotted line) while you press the back of the plane against your work surface.* Fold the belly from side to side a few times. As you did with the Jet, pull up the nose and pinch the fuselage together.

side view

1⅓"

*NOTE: This will properly align the tail and the wings.

1"

31

After you have pulled up the nose, line it up with the back. Then fold the wings up. You can now push the tail fin up.

32

With the tail pulled up, the plane should look like this.

33

Make another fold as
shown here for the
engine.

34

The finished version of
the Shuttle.

SPACE SHUTTLE

FUTURE FIGHTER

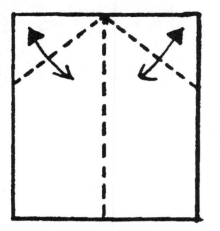

1

Fold the paper in half.
Unfold it, then fold down
the two corners.

2

Fold down on the
dotted line.

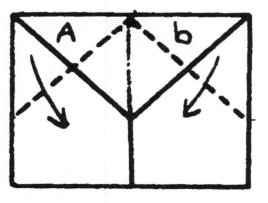

3

Fold the corners
diagonally again.

4

Your fold should look like this. Now, unfold the corners again.

5

Put your hand under the Side B fold, then lift and reverse the fold to the left, as shown.

6

The fold should look like this.

7

Now do the same to the other side. This is how it should look.

NOTE: These are the two front stabilizers.

8

Now, open at the center as shown here. Fold Sides F & E diagonally up as indicated.

open

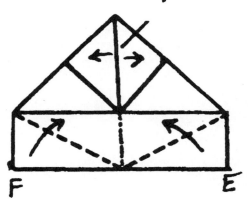

9

The folds of the lower corners should look like this. Tuck the corners under Sides A & B as shown here.

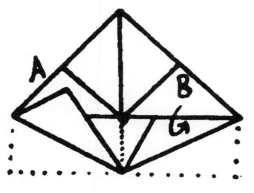

10

After you have tucked both corners under Sides A & B respectively, flip the stabilizers to the left side and make a fold on the dotted line toward the middle. Repeat on the left side.

stabilizers

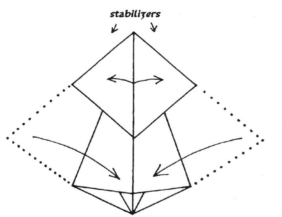

11

After you have folded both sides toward the middle and separated the two stabilizers, it should look like this.

12

Fold the right wing out along the dotted line as indicated.

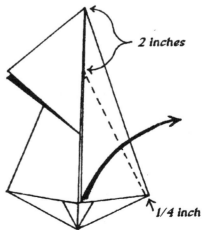

2 inches

1/4 inch

13

The folded right wing should look like this. Do the same thing on the left side before going on.

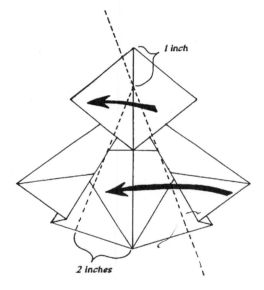

1 inch

2 inches

14

Fold the right side to the left along the dotted lines indicated by the arrows.

NOTE: Use the technique you learned with the Concord to complete the plane.

15

This is how the fold from Step 14 should look. Do the same on the left side.

NOTE: This new fold is great for compact planes when you don't fold the nose down first.

16

After you fold both sides, push the fuselage downward.

push

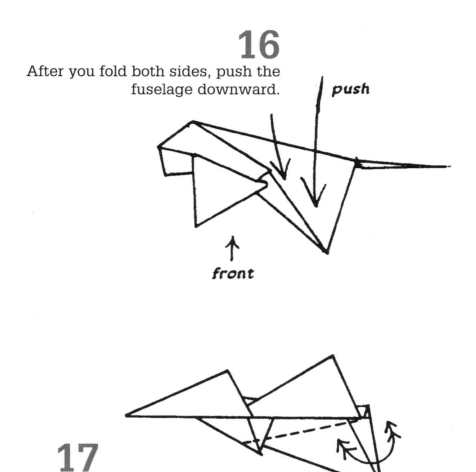

front

17

After you have pushed the
tail down, press the two sides together.
Fold the wings up, then fold the tail back
and forth along the dotted lines. Now
push inward and up.

18

This is how the plane looks
with the tail up.

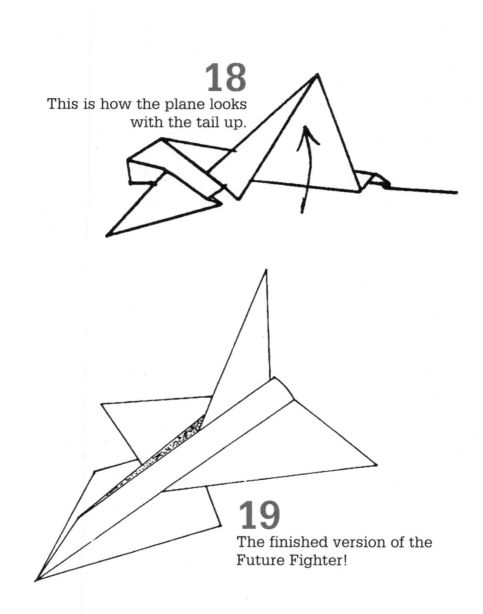

19

The finished version of the
Future Fighter!

FUTURE FIGHTER

The F-15 will repeat some of the same steps and folds as the Jet, so many of these first steps should seem familiar.

(NOTE: Make sure you've mastered the F-15 Eagle before folding the F-14 Tomcat.)

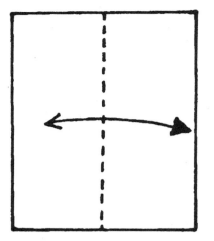

1
Fold paper in half,
then unfold.

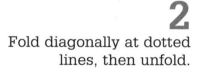

2
Fold diagonally at dotted
lines, then unfold.

3
Now, use both hands and
fold the paper up and in
toward the middle.

4

This is how the paper should look. Gently press down from the top.

5

Now, it should look like this.

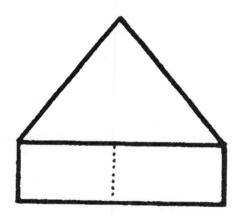

6

Slide your right hand under Flap X as shown here.

7

Flip Flap X over and onto Flap A.

8

Flap X should line up evenly with Flap A on the left side.

9

Now, fold Flap X on the dotted line toward the centerline.

10

This is how your fold
should look.

11

After you have folded
Flap X toward the middle
flap, flip it to the right
side. Notice the B edge.

12

This is how your plane
should look. Now, unfold &
flip the right wing to the
left side.

13

This is how it should look after you've flipped it to the left. Now fold on the dotted line so that Corner X meets Corner H.

14

This is how Step 13 should look. Repeat this fold on the left side.

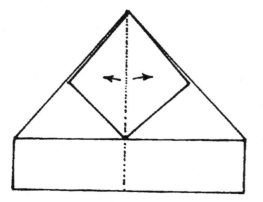

15

After you fold the left side, open both sides as indicated here.

16

Now open the wings further. The front wings now have two intersecting crease lines. Label them P and O.

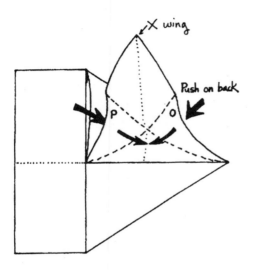

17

Rotate your paper ¼ turn to the right and fold P & O together and toward you on the crossing crease lines.

18

Your folds on P & O should look exactly as shown here. Put your hand behind the wing at M & N and press the two sides together.

19

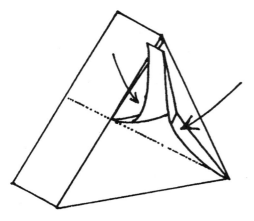

After pressing sides M & N together, this is how your plane should look. Do the same on the left side, beginning with Step 16, before going on.

20

Your finished folds of the wing should look like this. Fold the wing up toward the nose exactly as the arrow indicates.

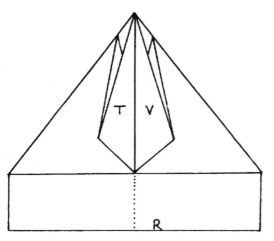

21

After you have finished with the other side, separate both sides as displayed. (Notice the R edge.)

22

Fold up the R edge at the midpoint, along the dotted line.

23

Now, fold back along the dotted line.

24

This is how your fold toward the back should look. Now unfold it as shown, so that it looks like the end of step 22.

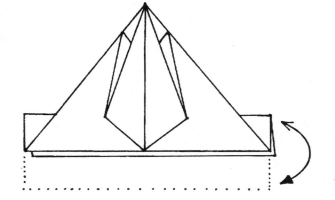

25

Fold diagonally up, then back and forth at each corner, as shown here.

26

This is how the folds on step 25 should look. Fold back and forth five or six times.

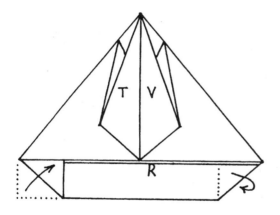

27

After you've folded the corners, unfold the R edge fold as shown. You should have two triangular shapes.

28

Push the two triangular sides inward as shown.

29

After you have pressed both triangular sides inward, it should look like this. Now, fold this part back on the dotted line. Next, flip the V wing to the T wing on the left side.

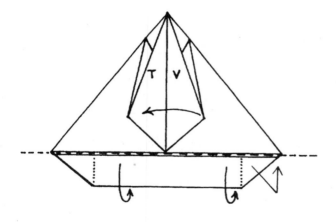

30

Now, fold Edge B to Centerline C on the dotted line. Do the same to the left side.

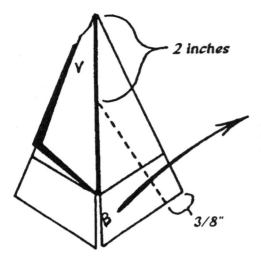

31

Fold Edge B to the right on the dotted line.

32

This is how your fold should look. Fold the left side the same way. Now fold the right side toward the center as shown.

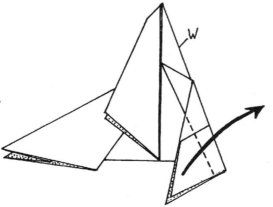

33

The fold from Step 32 should be parallel to Edge Line W. Now, make another fold on the dotted line toward the outside.

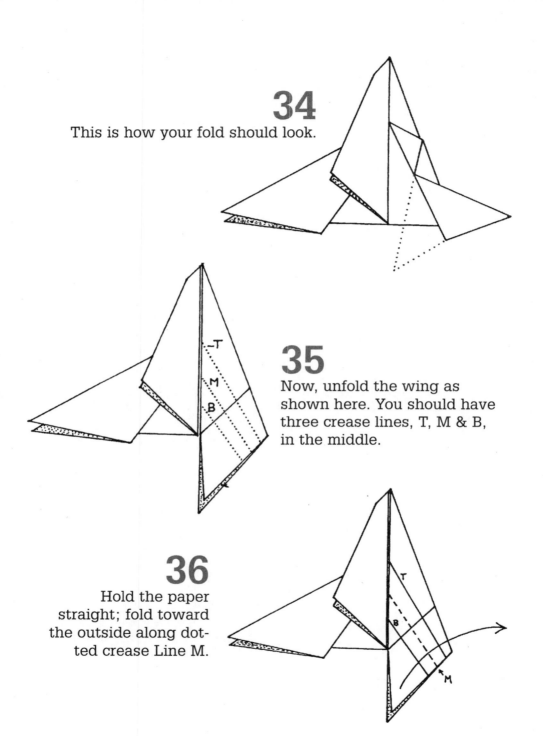

34

This is how your fold should look.

35

Now, unfold the wing as shown here. You should have three crease lines, T, M & B, in the middle.

36

Hold the paper straight; fold toward the outside along dotted crease Line M.

37

Your fold should look like this. Again, fold Edge M to Edge W.

38

This is how the fold from Step 37 should look.

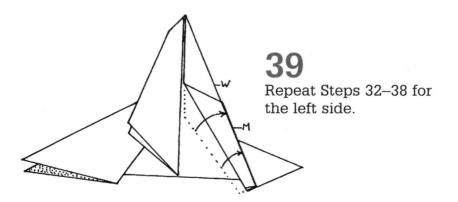

39

Repeat Steps 32–38 for the left side.

40

Now, separate the two front wings so that the plane looks like this.

inside right wing

right wing

41

Fold the inside right wing to match the angle of the right stabilizer (see Step 42). Do the same to the inside left wing.

42

Match the angle of the front wing to the stabilizer. Do the same to the other side.

1¼" inches

2¹/² inches

43

This is what your plane should look like.

44

Now, fold the right side to the left and fold the left side to the right.

45

Now, open the folds; you should have two crease lines.

crease

46

After you have folded the two sides, you should be able to push the belly downward without losing the sharp nose.

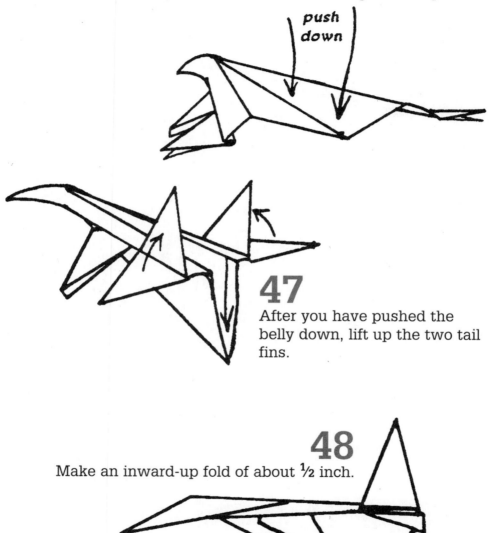

push down

47

After you have pushed the belly down, lift up the two tail fins.

48

Make an inward-up fold of about ½ inch.

1⁴ inches

3/4 inches

49

From the rear, the plane should look like this.

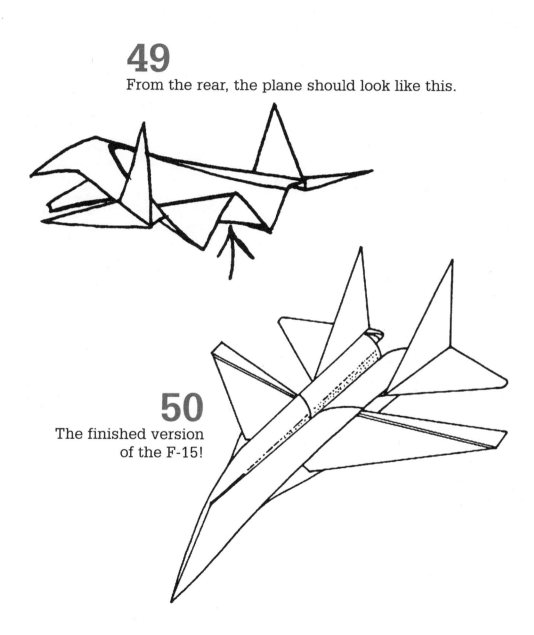

50

The finished version
of the F-15!

F-15 EAGLE

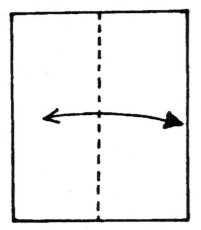

1

Fold paper in half, then unfold.

2

Fold diagonally at dotted lines, then unfold.

3

Now, use both hands and fold the paper up and in toward the middle.

4

This is how the paper should look. Gently press down from the top.

5

Now, it should look like this.

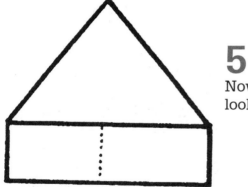

6

Slide your right hand under Flap X as shown here.

7

Flip Flap X over
and onto Flap A.

8

Flap X should line up
evenly with Flap A on
the left side.

9

Now, fold Flap X on
the dotted line
toward the centerline.

10

This is how your fold should look.

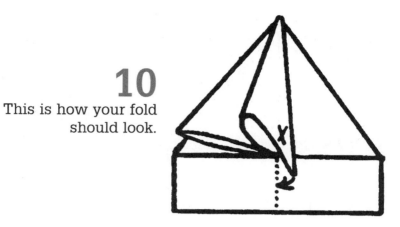

11

After you have folded Flap X toward the middle flap, flip it to the right side. Notice the B Edge.

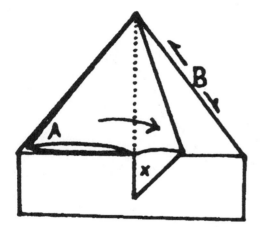

12

This is how your plane should look. Now, unfold & flip the right wing to the left side.

13

This is how it should look after you've flipped it to the left. Now fold on the dotted line so that Corner X meets Corner H.

14

This is how Step 13 should look. Repeat this fold on the left side.

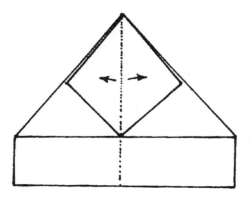

15

After you fold the left side, open both sides as indicated here.

16

Now open the wings further. The front wings now have two intersecting crease lines. Label them P and O.

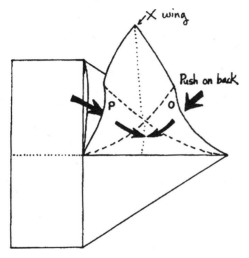

17

Rotate your paper ¼ turn to the right and fold P & O together and toward you on the crossing crease lines.

18

Your folds on P & O should look exactly as shown here. Put your hand behind the wing at M & N and press the two sides together.

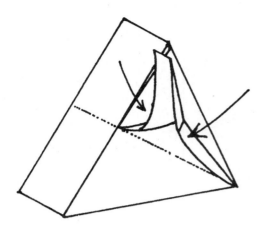

19

After pressing sides M & N together, this is how your plane should look. Do the same on the left side, beginning with Step 16, before going on.

20

Your finished folds of the wing should look like this. Fold the wing up toward the nose exactly as the arrow indicates.

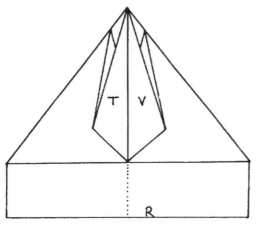

21

After you have finished with the other side, separate both sides as displayed. (Notice the R edge.)

22

Fold up the R edge
at the midpoint,
along the dotted line.

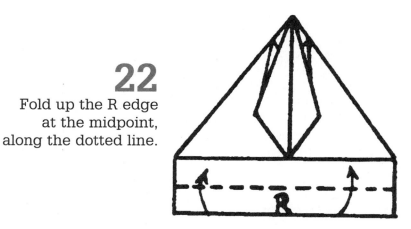

23

Now, fold back along
the dotted line.

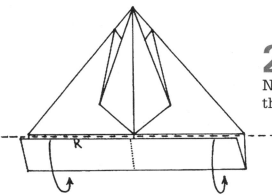

24

This is how your fold
toward the back should
look. Now unfold it as
shown, so that it looks
like the end of step 22.

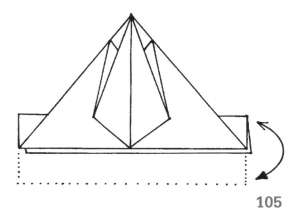

25

Fold diagonally up, then back and forth at each corner, as shown here.

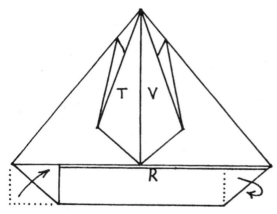

26

This is how the folds on step 25 should look. Fold back and forth five or six times.

27

After you've folded the corners, unfold the R edge fold as shown. You should have two triangular shapes.

28

Push the two triangular sides inward as shown.

29

After you have pressed both triangular sides inward, it should look like this. Now, fold this part back on the dotted line. Next, flip the V wing to the T wing on the left side.

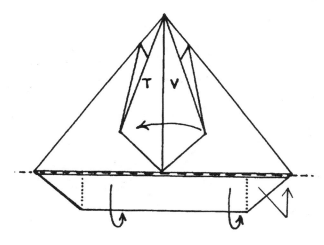

30

Now, fold Edge B to Centerline C on the dotted line. Do the same to the left side.

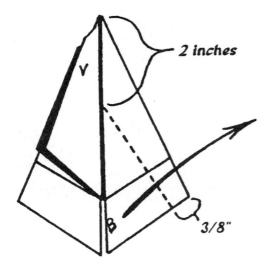

2 inches

3/8"

31
Fold Edge B to the right on the dotted line.

32
Your plane should look like this. Fold the front stabilizer straight to the left side as shown by the top arrow.

NOTE: The left side has not been folded toward the middle in this drawing.

33
This is how the fold should look.

34

This is how your fully folded stabilizer should look. Flip the right stabilizer to the right and do the same on the other side.

35

After you've finished both sides, separate them as shown.

36

Fold on the dotted lines, as indicated. Fold the right side to the left and the left side to the right exactly as on the F-15.

NOTE: Work on a flat surface.

37

This is how your fold to the left side should look. Press hard on the fold, then unfold it and do the same on the left side.

38

After you've folded the two sides of the plane, open it up. You should see two crease lines (as shown by the dotted lines.)

39

Now, turn your plane over, with the belly down. Press the centerline down as indicated by the arrows until the two sides come close together. With your thumb and fingers, press the plane's fuselage tightly together.

front

40
This is how your plane
should look from the side.

41
Now fold the wings up.

42
Fold up the two tail wings as shown.

43
The finished version
of the Stealth-X!

BOMBER

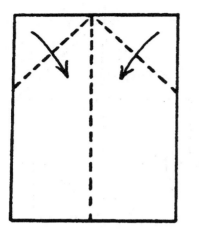

1

Fold the paper in half.
Then open it and fold the
two top corners toward
the centerline.

This is how your folds should
look. Now make the bottom
folds at the corners, as
indicated.

2

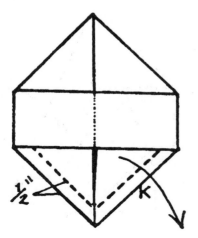

3

This is how the folds on the four
corners should look. Make a
downward-out fold as indicated,
leaving about ½ inch.

4

This is how your
downward-out fold
should look.

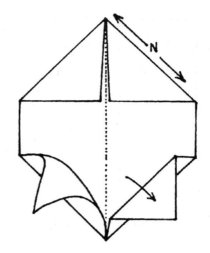

5

Now, fold Edge N on the
dotted line to the centerline.

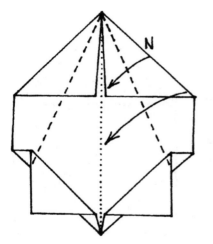

6

This is how your N Line
fold toward the centerline
should look. Do the same
to the other side.

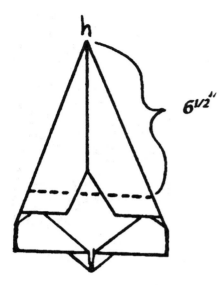

7

The plane should now look like this. Next, measure 6½ inches from H and fold down along the dotted line.

8

This is how the fold should look. Now, fold up on the dotted line, which should be about 1 inch from Line D.

9

Now the plane should look like this. Fold Edge V to the centerline.

10

This is how your fold toward the centerline should look. Open it back up and do the same on the other side.

11

After you open it up again, close it and put your left hand over the G spots and open the lower part of the wing with your right hand.

12

You should be able to spot a pocket where you see the A. Stick your finger in as shown and place your left thumb above the pocket where the C is shown.

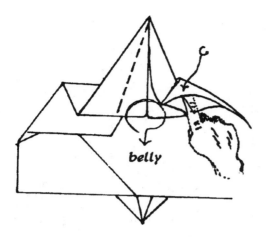

13

Gently, press down from the top of the pocket; it should close easily.

14

After pressing down both pockets, the plane should look like this. (Notice the ¾" wing edge.) Fold the indicated edges under the wings and belly as shown by the arrows.

3/4"

15

The B corner should be folded directly under the belly. It should look exactly like the left finished side on the diagram. This is a very important step.

16

After you have folded the two parts under the belly, your plane should look exactly as shown. Now, 2½ inches down from H, fold along the dotted line.

17

This is how your fold should look.

18

After you have folded the nose down, fold the two sides of the plane toward the back so that it looks like this from the side view. Then, lift up the nose.

19

Hold your right hand under the plane as shown and, with your left hand, pull up the nose of the plane.

20

After you have pulled up the nose, carefully line up the plane's back so that it looks exactly as shown here.

21

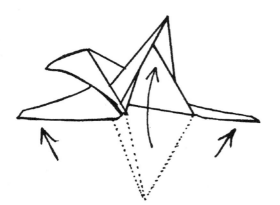

Now, lift up the plane's wings so that they are flat and even. Then lift the tail fin as indicated. Fold the wings back down and press hard on them from both sides of the fuselage. Finally, lift the wings up again and you're done.

121

22
The finished version
of the Bomber!

123

STAR FIGHTER

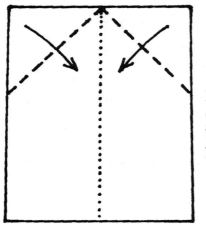

1

Fold the paper in half and open it back up. Fold the top two corners toward the middle line.

2

Your folds should look like this.

3

Fold up along the dotted line.

4
Your fold should
look like this.

5
Fold down Edge C
at the midpoint.

6
Your fold should
look like this.

7

Unfold Edge E.

8

Make two upward folds from the two bottom corners as shown, along the diagonal dotted lines.

9

This is how your bottom corner folds should look. Fold back and forth four to five times at each corner.

127

10

Open the corners as shown. Then fold the bottom edge line B upward, along the dotted line.

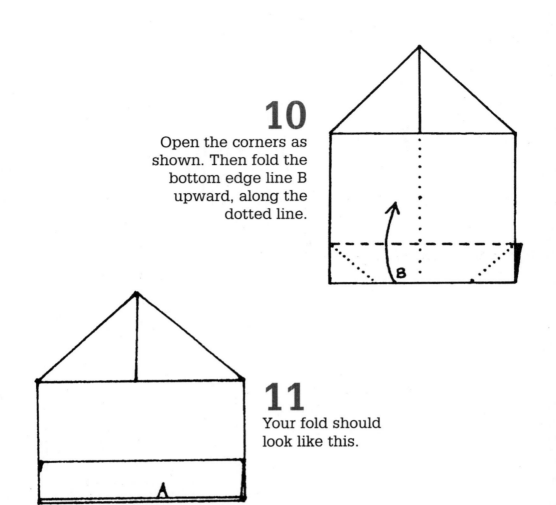

11

Your fold should look like this.

12

Lift Edge A halfway up, as shown. Now you should have a triangular shape on each side. Push both triangular shapes inward and toward each other.

13

This is how it should look.
Now fold the right fin as
indicated to the left side
on the dotted line. Do the
same on the left side.

14

Your fold to the center
should look like this.

15

Now, unfold to the outside
as indicated.

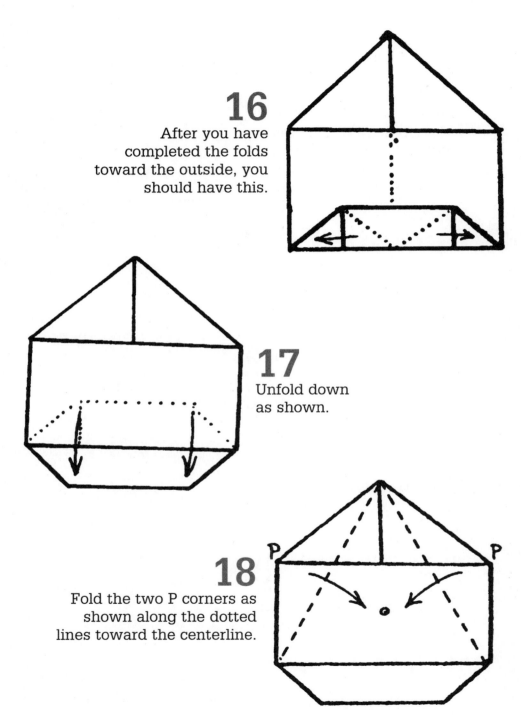

16
After you have
completed the folds
toward the outside, you
should have this.

17
Unfold down
as shown.

18
Fold the two P corners as
shown along the dotted
lines toward the centerline.

P

P

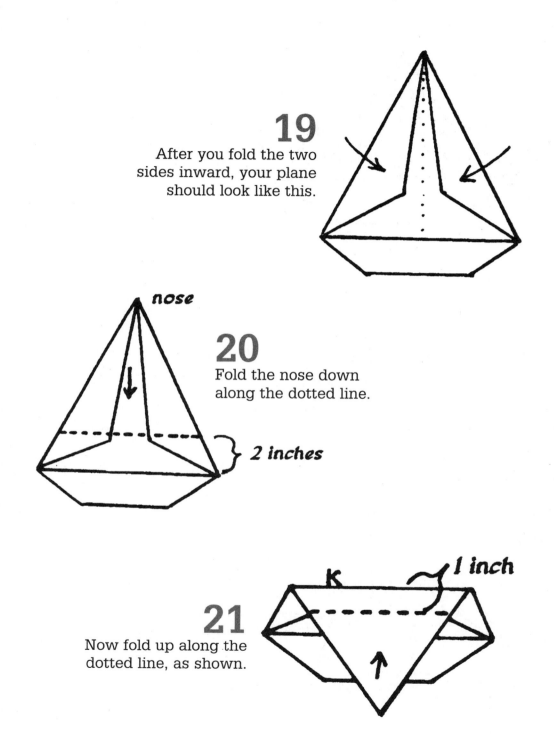

19

After you fold the two sides inward, your plane should look like this.

20

Fold the nose down along the dotted line.

nose

2 inches

21

Now fold up along the dotted line, as shown.

K

1 inch

131

22

Your fold should
look like this.

23

Now fold Edge X
toward the centerline.

NOTE: The intent of this fold
is to get two triangular
shapes in Step 27.

x

X

24

This is how your fold
should look. Now
unfold it and repeat
on the other side.

25

After you have unfolded the sides, you should have a little pocket behind the X. Put your index finger inside and your thumb on the X, as indicated by the arrows.

26

Simply place your left hand over the A's while your right finger and thumb press the pocket downward to look like Step 27.

27

You should now have two upside-down triangular shapes. Yours may look a bit different, but carry on.

28

Now, fold both sides diagonally down as shown, along the dotted lines.

29

This is how the folds should look.

30

Fold up the lower part along dotted Line F.

31

This is how your
fold should look.

32

Now, fold the nose down
along the dotted line
(about two inches down).

2 inches

33

This is how your fold
should look. Now fold
the whole plane back
and together, in half.

34

This is how the fold toward the back should look from the side. Next, lift up the nose and pinch along the belly about one inch up.

NOTE: For the best results, always place the plane's back against a flat surface.

35

This is how the plane should look after you've lifted the nose and aligned the fuselage. The tiny Line M should be about 1/4 inch long.

← M

36

Now, lift up the wings as shown.

37

Separate the edges of each wing into two sides and fold them back and forth.

38

This is how your plane should look.

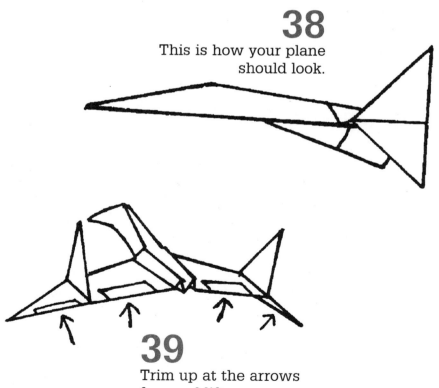

39

Trim up at the arrows for good lift.

OPTION: Make cuts for flaps for easier flying.

40
The finished version of the Star Fighter!

41
You can also open the tail fins to make the rocket boosters appear.

STAR FIGHTER

F-117 NIGHTHAWK

In making the Nighthawk, be careful and precise when you tear and tuck the wing inward.

NOTE: This technique will also be necessary for the MIG-27.

1

Fold the paper in half,
then open it back up.

1¼ inch

2

Fold it down about
1¼" from the top.

3

Your fold should
look like this.

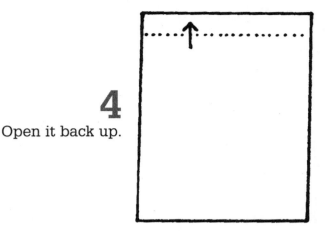

4

Open it back up.

5

Turn your paper sideways. Fold the top right corner diagonally down to the left crease line as indicated.

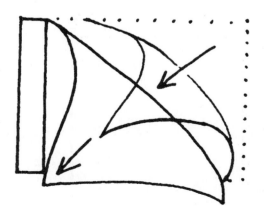

6

Fold from the top right corner.

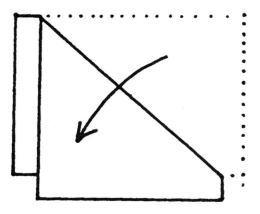

7

It should look
like this.

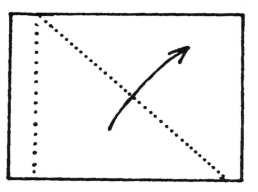

8

Now, open it
back up.

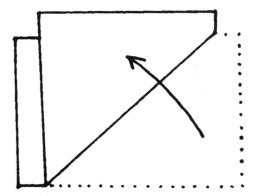

9

Make a fold from the
lower right-hand
corner diagonally up
and left as shown.

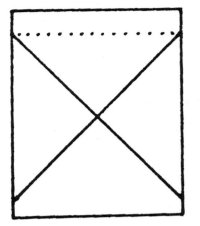

10

Open it back up, rotate your paper a quarter turn and you should have the crossing lines you see here.

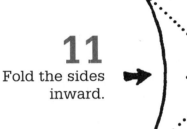

11

Fold the sides inward.

12

Your inward fold should look like this.

13

Press down and it should look like this. The base might not be even, but don't worry about it.

14

Flip Fin B to the left side.

15

Make a fold toward the middle line as shown by the arrows.

16

Your fold should look like this.

17

Do the same on the left side.

2³/⁴ inches

18

Flip Flaps A & B to the left. Fold outward along the dotted line.

19
Your fold should look like this.

B

20
Fold Edge C to Edge D.

B

C

D

1/2 inch

21
Your fold should look like this. Do the same on the left side.

B

22

Now, turn the paper over so that you can see how the back looks.

back side

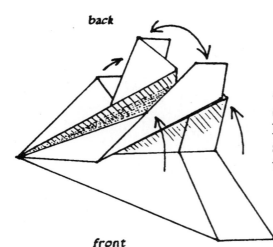

back

front

23

Raise the two folded sides and make sure they're even.

front

$2^{1/2}$ inches

24

Turn the plane over and make a tear about 2½ inches long as indicated here.

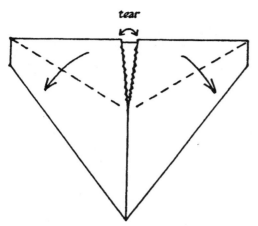

25

Your tear should look like this. Fold the two sides as indicated.

NOTE: Cutting is optional.

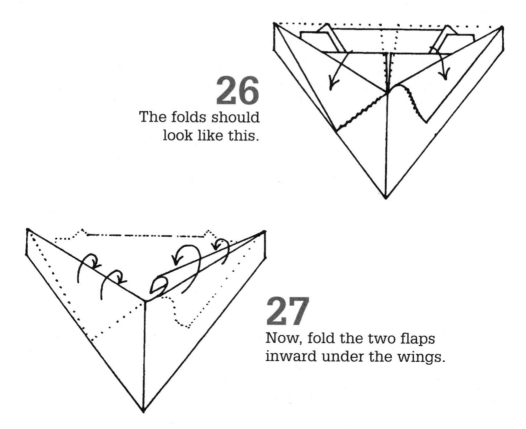

26

The folds should look like this.

27

Now, fold the two flaps inward under the wings.

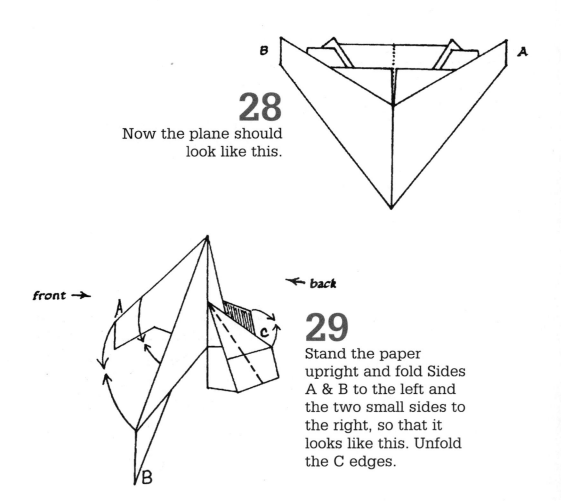

28

Now the plane should look like this.

29

Stand the paper upright and fold Sides A & B to the left and the two small sides to the right, so that it looks like this. Unfold the C edges.

30

Your plane should look like this. Make a small fold up on the bottom as indicated, on the top flap only. Do the same on the other side.

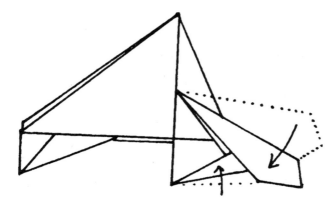

31

Now, fold the upper portion of the tail fin down. Do the same on the other side.

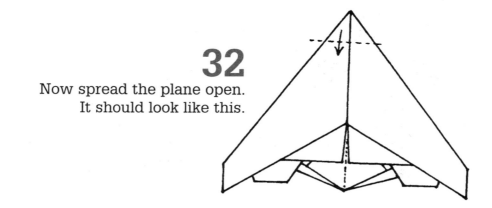

32

Now spread the plane open. It should look like this.

33

Fold the nose down toward you about one inch from the top.

34

With your hand in the position shown, turn the plane sideways.

NOTE: Remember this procedure from previous airplanes.

35

Now, grip the belly with your left hand and use your right hand to line up the back, then press the two sides down, as shown in this top view.

36

This is how your plane should look after you have folded the two sides down.

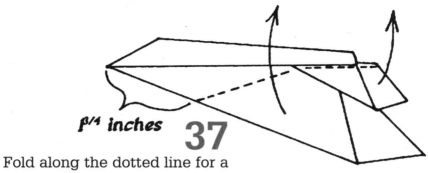

p/4 inches ## 37

Fold along the dotted line for a
more authentic looking plane.

flying version

38

From the side,
your plane should
now look like this.
Fold the wings up
as indicated & do
the same on the
other side.

39

This is how the plane should
look after you have folded the
four wings up. Make
sure they're even.

1 ¾ inch

40

Make an inward-up fold as indicated, similar to the ones you have made on earlier planes in this book.

side view

back view

tail view

41

Lift up and widen the two sides as indicated by the arrows.

42

The finished version
of the Nighthawk!

paper clip

Flying Version

43

To fly this plane, place a paper clip as shown, and tightly press the nose to make it pointed. Slide the paper clip back & forth for balance. Throw the plane straight out from your body and it should fly and glide smoothly.

F-117 NIGHTHAWK

MIG-27 FLOGGER

You will not be able to make this plane until you have mastered both the Nighthawk and the Jet. In making the MIG-27, after a few initial folds, you'll find yourself repeating some steps that you learned making the F-117 Nighthawk and a few steps from the Jet.

157

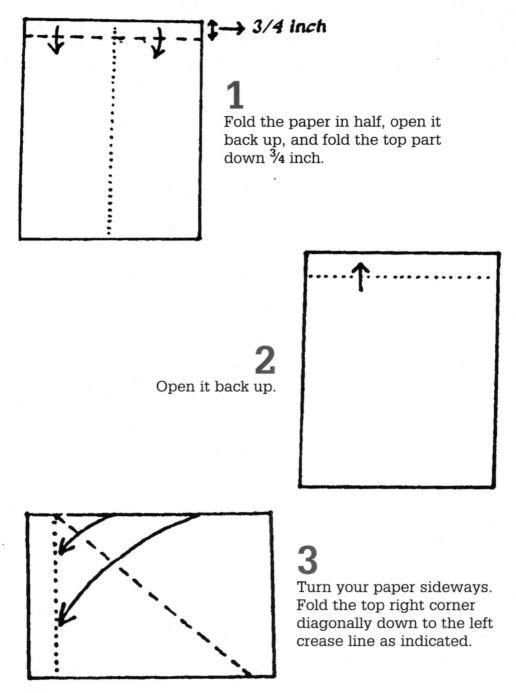

3/4 inch

1

Fold the paper in half, open it back up, and fold the top part down ¾ inch.

2

Open it back up.

3

Turn your paper sideways. Fold the top right corner diagonally down to the left crease line as indicated.

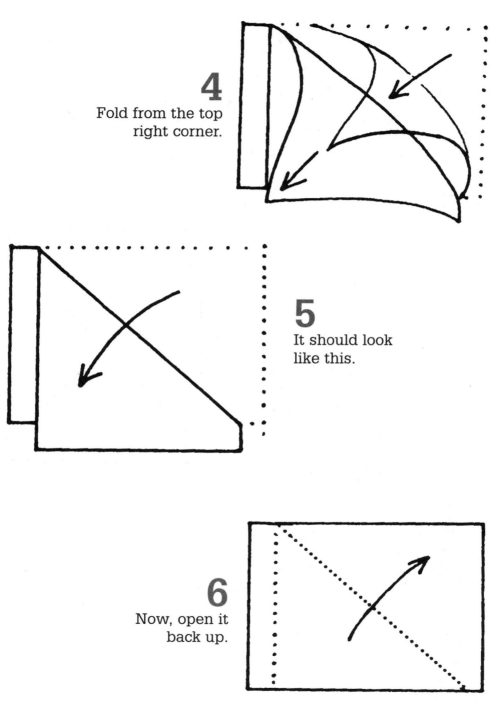

4 Fold from the top right corner.

5 It should look like this.

6 Now, open it back up.

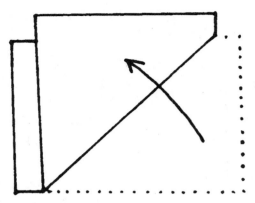

7

Make a fold from the lower right-hand corner diagonally up and left as shown.

8

Open it back up, rotate your paper a quarter turn and you should have the crossing lines you see here.

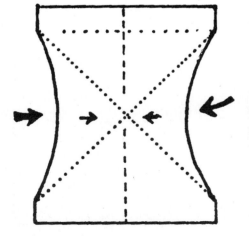

9

Fold the sides inward.

10

Your inward fold should look like this.

11

Press down and it should look like this. The base might not be even, but don't worry about it.

12

Flip Fin B to the left side.

13

Make a fold toward the middle line as shown by the arrows.

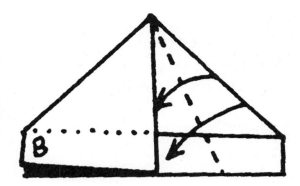

14

Your fold should look like this.

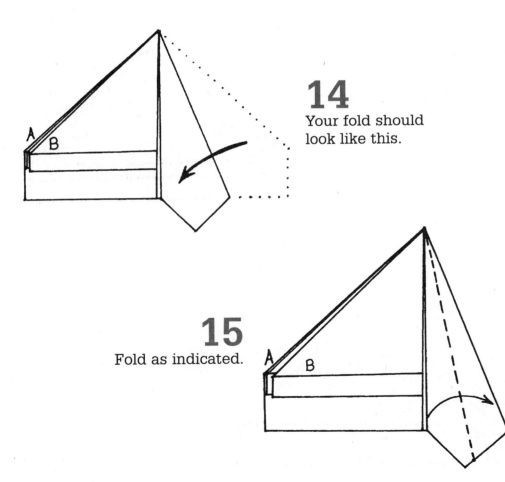

15

Fold as indicated.

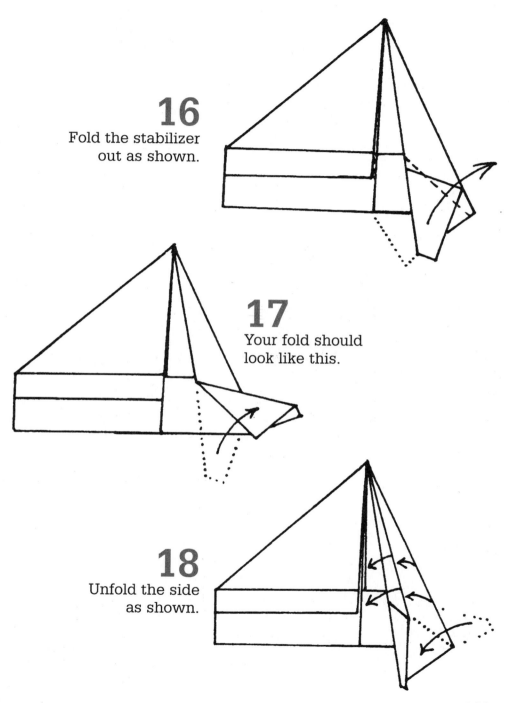

16
Fold the stabilizer
out as shown.

17
Your fold should
look like this.

18
Unfold the side
as shown.

19

Your plane should now look like this.

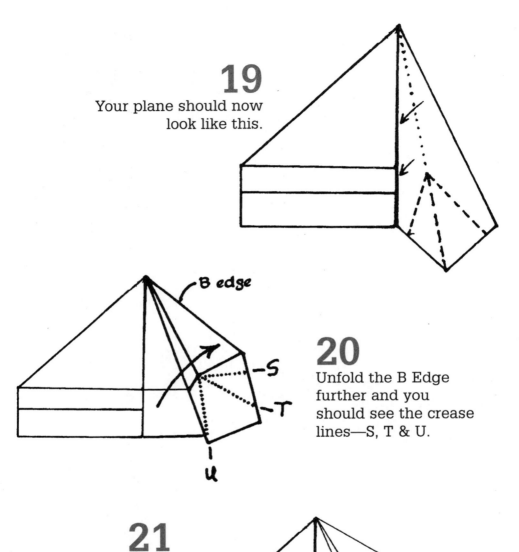

20

Unfold the B Edge further and you should see the crease lines—S, T & U.

B edge

S

T

U

21

Put your index finger on the middle of Line T and push it outward while pushing Lines S & U inward as indicated by the arrows.

S

T

U

22
Your plane should look like this after you push out Line T. Press down on Point A.

23
Your inward-out fold should look like this. Repeat Steps 20–24 on the left side.

24
Open up the plane so it looks like this.

25

Make a tear as you did with the Nighthawk, and like the Nighthawk, fold toward the inside.

26

Your inside fold should look like this. (Notice the L left wing & R right wing.)

27

Fold the R wing toward the middle line.

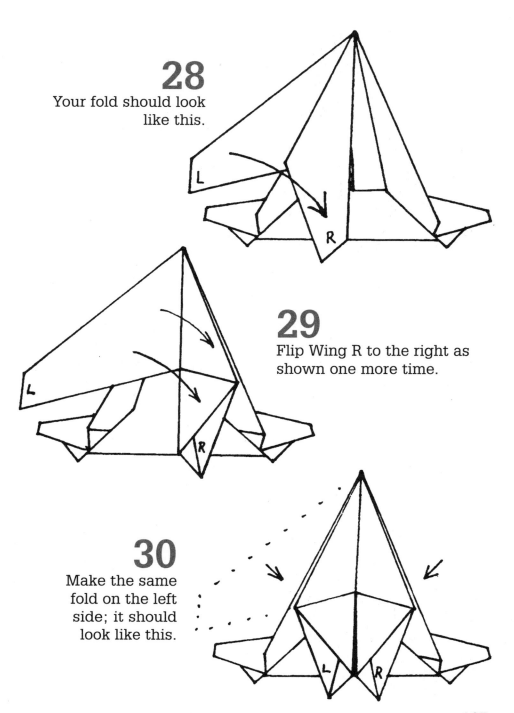

28
Your fold should look
like this.

29
Flip Wing R to the right as
shown one more time.

30
Make the same
fold on the left
side; it should
look like this.

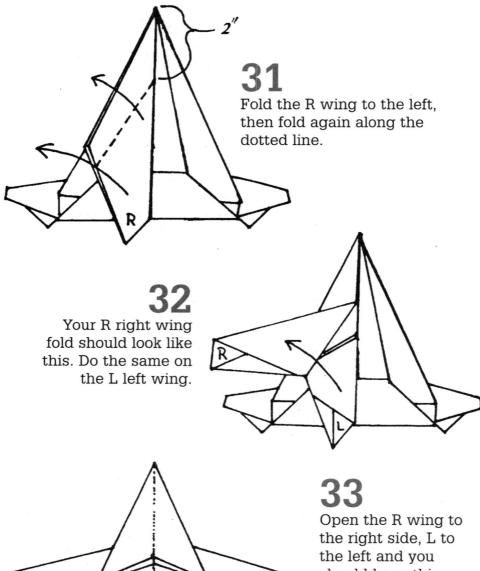

31

Fold the R wing to the left, then fold again along the dotted line.

32

Your R right wing fold should look like this. Do the same on the L left wing.

33

Open the R wing to the right side, L to the left and you should have this. Now, fold the nose down and finish the plane. If you have trouble, go on to the next step.

34

Measure about 1¼ inches from the end of the nose. Fold down the nose along the dotted line.

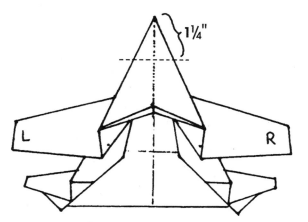

35

Your fold should look like this.

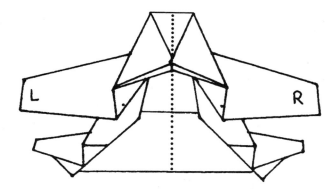

36

After folding down the nose, fold both sides of the plane's body toward the back as shown.

37

From the side, your plane should look like this. Now, hold the body with your left hand, and, with the other, pull up the nose. Then, as you did on the Concord (Steps 17–20), lay the plane, upside down, on a flat surface and fold the under fuselage back and forth. Notice the 2-inch depth.

2″

38

Continue to grip the plane firmly in your left hand while using the thumb and index finger of your right hand to press hard along the plane's body, as shown here.

Press hard together

39

Move your right hand under the wings.

← slide →

40

Carefully apply pressure while sliding your left hand along the back of the plane.

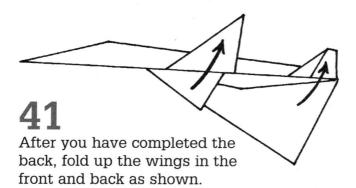

41

After you have completed the back, fold up the wings in the front and back as shown.

1³/₄'

42

Fold along the dotted line four times from side to side.

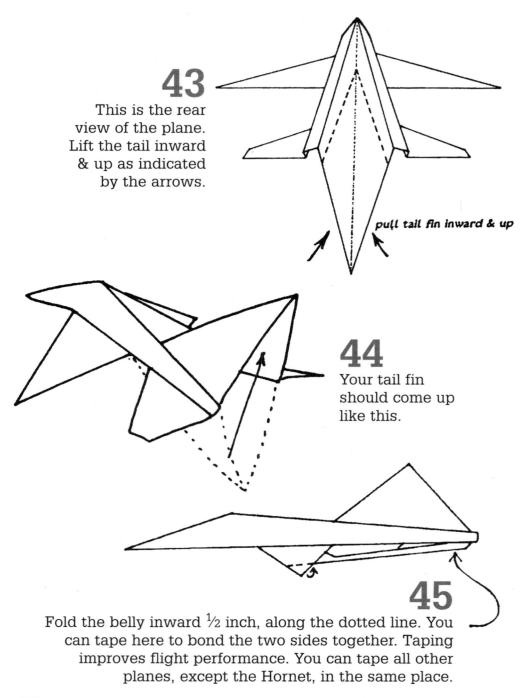

43

This is the rear
view of the plane.
Lift the tail inward
& up as indicated
by the arrows.

pull tail fin inward & up

44

Your tail fin
should come up
like this.

45

Fold the belly inward ½ inch, along the dotted line. You
can tape here to bond the two sides together. Taping
improves flight performance. You can tape all other
planes, except the Hornet, in the same place.

46

The finished version
of the Jet.

47

Curve the side of
the nose for a nice,
round, clean, front
end like the one in
Diagram B.

cut under this fold

cut away

48

You are now finished with the MIG. If you want the tail to
look more realistic, pull it down the way it was before you
raised it, then cut along the dotted lines and push it back
up. Make sure that it's even with the body.

fold inward

49

Bring the tail up like this.

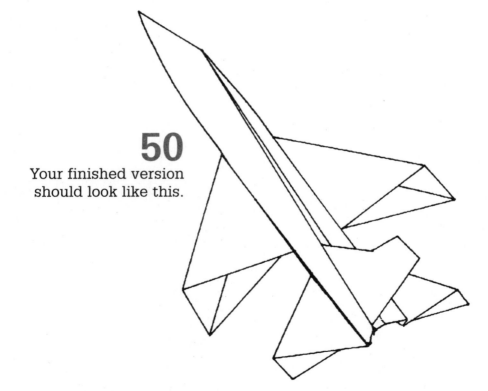

50

Your finished version
should look like this.

MIG-27 FLOGGER

SAAB 37 VIGGEN

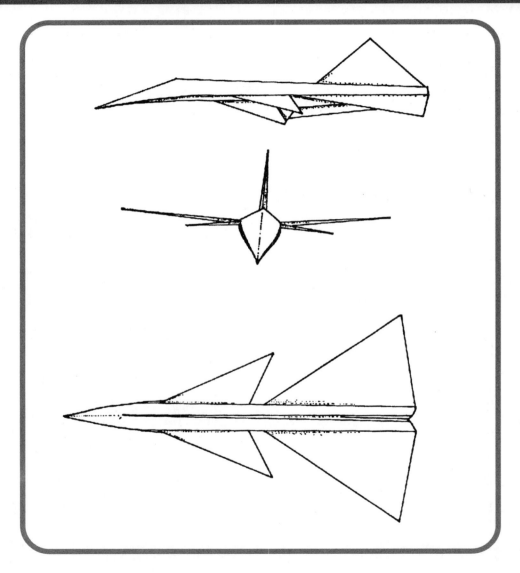

The Saab 37 Viggen also uses many of the folds
that you learned making the Jet.

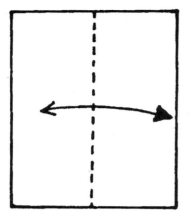

1

Fold paper in half,
then unfold.

2

Fold diagonally at
dotted lines, then
unfold.

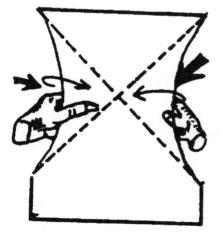

3

Now, use both hands and
fold the paper up and in
toward the middle.

4

This is how the paper should look. Gently press down from the top.

5

Now, it should look like this.

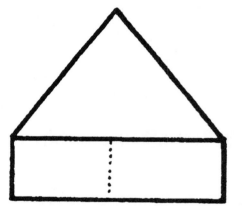

6

Slide your right hand under Flap X as shown here.

7

Flip Flap X over
and onto Flap A.

8

Flap X should line up
evenly with Flap A on
the left side.

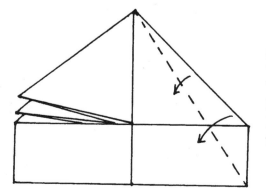

9

Your plane should
look like this.
Make a fold on
the dotted line.

10

Your fold should
look like this.

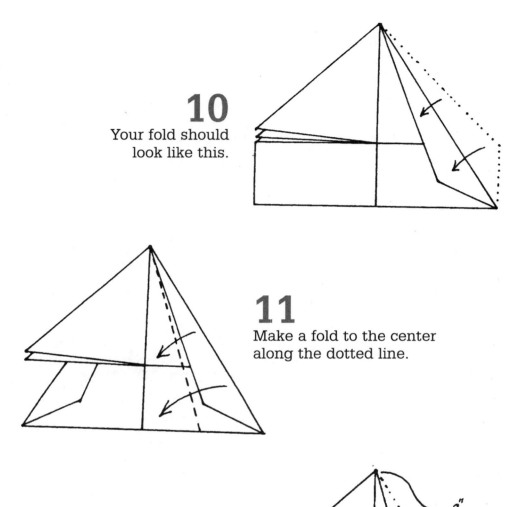

11

Make a fold to the center
along the dotted line.

12

Make another fold
along the dotted line.

3"

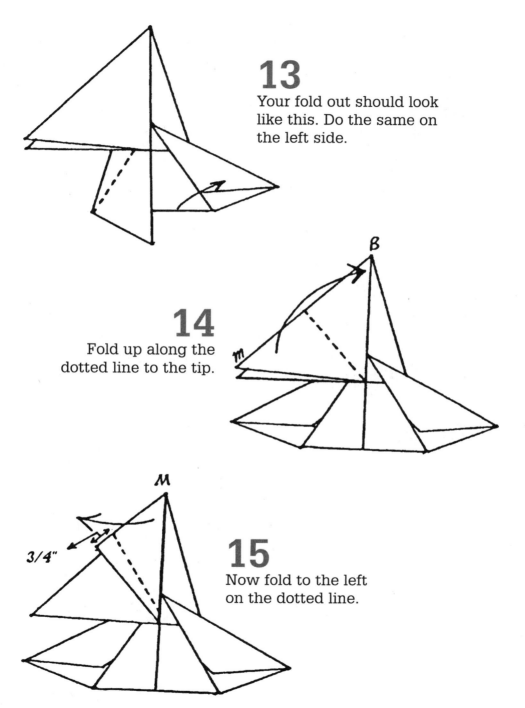

13

Your fold out should look like this. Do the same on the left side.

14

Fold up along the dotted line to the tip.

15

Now fold to the left on the dotted line.

16

Your fold to the left side should look like this. Repeat Steps 14 & 15 to the left side, (Fold Edge A to the right, even with Edge B.)

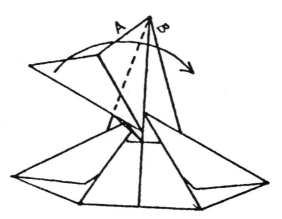

17

Your fold to the right should look like this. Now fold Edge K to the right so it's even with Edge B.

18

Your completed fold of Edge K should turn out like this.

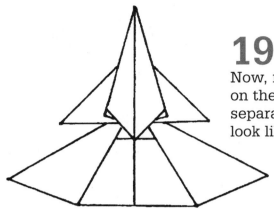

19

Now, repeat Steps 16–18 on the left side, and then separate the sides. It should look like this.

20

Measure about 1¼ inches from the end of the nose. Fold down the nose along the dotted line.

1¼ inch

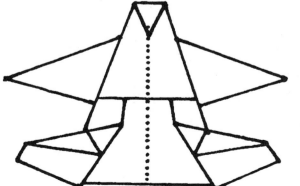

21

Your fold should look like this.

22

After folding down the nose, fold both sides of the plane's body toward the back as shown.

23

2"

From the side, your plane should look like this. Now, hold the body with your left hand, and, with the other, pull up the nose. Then, as you did on the Concord (Steps 17–20), lay the plane, upside down, on a flat surface and fold the under fuselage back and forth. Notice the 2-inch depth.

24

Continue to grip the plane firmly in your left hand while using the thumb and index finger of your right hand to press hard along the plane's body, as shown here.

Press hard together

25
Move your right hand under
the wings.

← slide →

26
Carefully apply pressure while sliding your left
hand along the back of the plane.

27
After you have completed the back,
fold up the wings in the front and
back as shown.

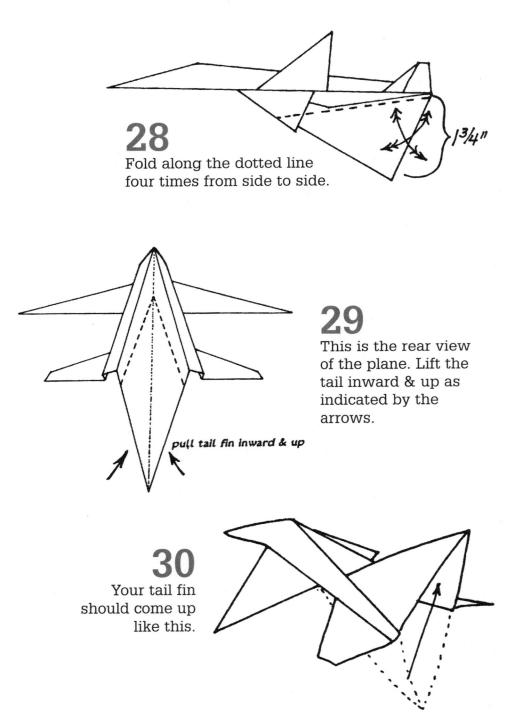

28
Fold along the dotted line
four times from side to side.

1¾"

29

This is the rear view
of the plane. Lift the
tail inward & up as
indicated by the
arrows.

pull tail fin inward & up

30
Your tail fin
should come up
like this.

31

Fold the belly inward ½ inch, along the dotted line.
You can tape here to bond the two sides together.
Taping improves flight performance. You can tape all
other planes, except the Hornet, in the same place.

32

The Viggen should
now look like this.

33

Curve the side of the
nose for a nice, round,
clean, front end like
the one in Diagram B.

A

B

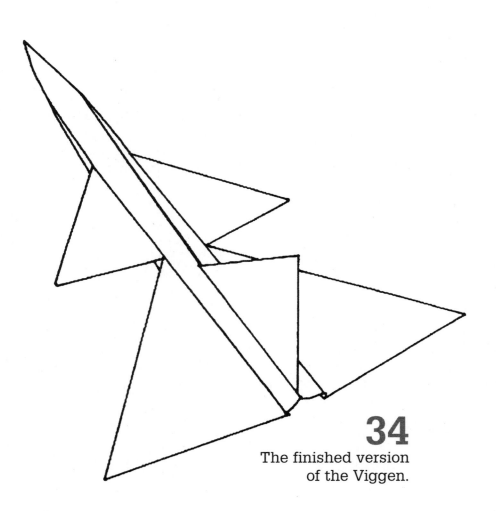

34
The finished version
of the Viggen.

F-18 HORNET

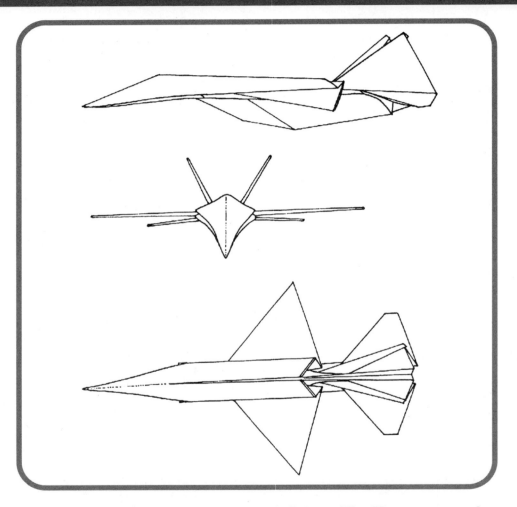

This is the U.S. F-18 Hornet, a unique fighter. The Hornet cannot be folded until you have mastered the Jet and the planes that follow. Like the real Hornet on which this plane is modeled, it will fly straight and fast. It's a tough plane, so be patient. You can ensure a compact and sturdy shape by making sure the folds are tight and accurate.

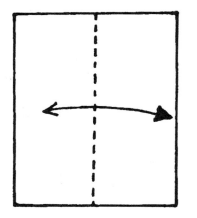

1

Fold paper in half,
then unfold.

2

Fold diagonally
at dotted lines,
then unfold.

3

Now, use both hands and
fold the paper up and in
toward the middle.

4

This is how the
paper should look.
Gently press down
from the top.

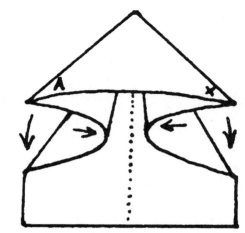

5

Now, it should
look like this.

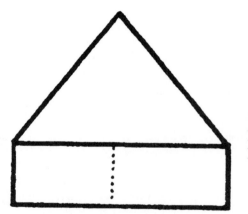

6

Slide your right hand
under Flap X as
shown here.

7

Flip Flap X over
and onto Flap A.

8

Flap X should line up
evenly with Flap A on
the left side.

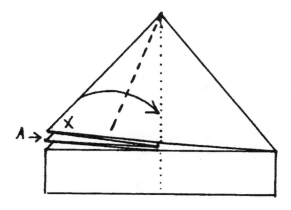

9

Now, fold Flap X on
the dotted line toward
the centerline.

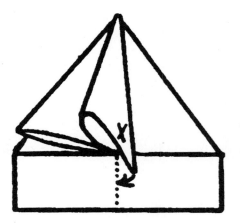

10

This is how your fold should look.

11

After you have folded Flap X toward the middle flap, flip it to the right side. Notice the B edge.

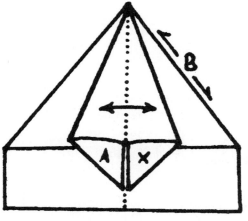

12

Now, repeat Steps 9–11 for the left side, and open the flaps to look like this.

13

Now, flip Flap X to the left, over Flap A again.

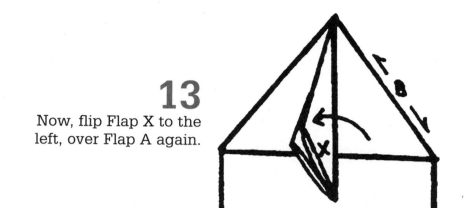

14

Measure about 1⅜ inches in at each side; fold toward the middle as indicated by the arrows.

15

Your folds should look like this.

NOTE: Back sides are Wings A & X.

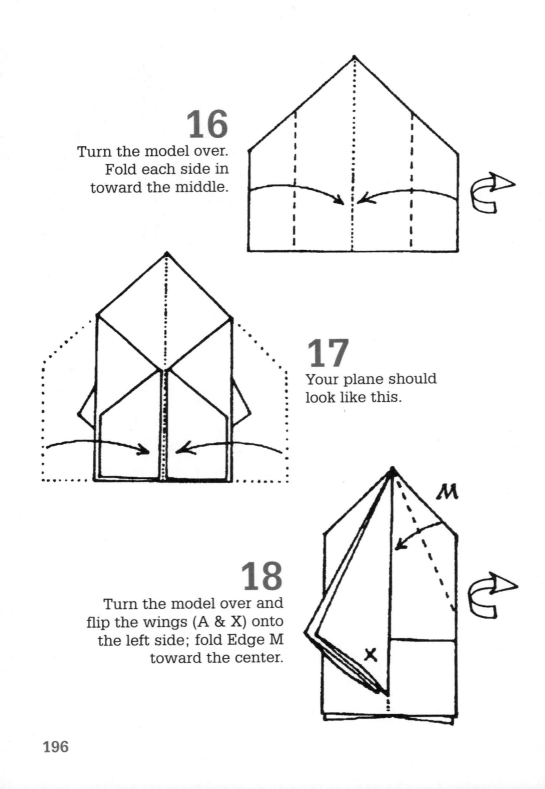

16

Turn the model over. Fold each side in toward the middle.

17

Your plane should look like this.

18

Turn the model over and flip the wings (A & X) onto the left side; fold Edge M toward the center.

19

It should look like this.
Do the same on the
left side.

20

This is what you
should have after
completing Steps 18
& 19 and separating
the two wings.

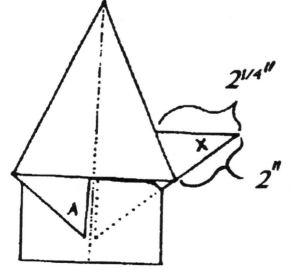

2¼"

2"

21

Pull the wings out
(using the technique
learned on earlier
planes). Do the same
to the left side.

22

Now your plane should look like this.

23

Turn the plane over; it will look like this. (The back now becomes the front.)

24

Fold the nose down and both sides of the body together. (You should remember how from previous planes.)

Pinch the sides tightly together & push the plane's wings open from the back.

25
Your plane should look like this.

Pinch sides together under the arrows

26
Your plane should look like this.

27
Side view.

28

Tail (back view). Push up, as you've done with the tail fins of previous planes.

3"

Tail (back view)

push up

29

Your plane should look like this.

30

Now, open up the wings and fold as indicated. Do one side first, then the other.

1/4"

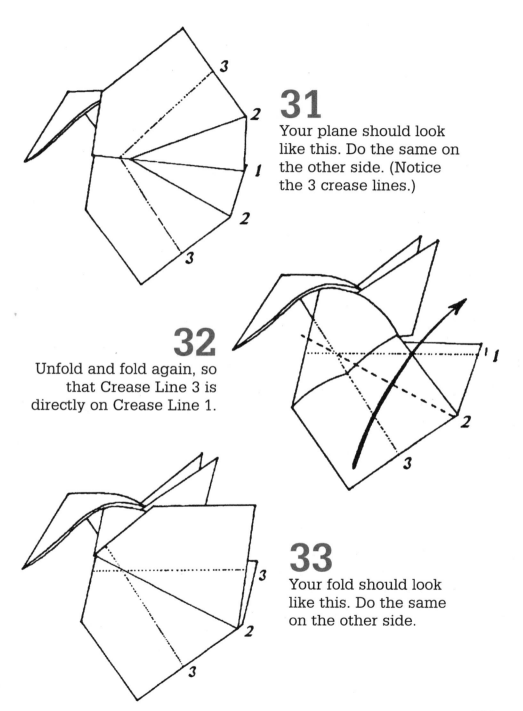

31

Your plane should look like this. Do the same on the other side. (Notice the 3 crease lines.)

32

Unfold and fold again, so that Crease Line 3 is directly on Crease Line 1.

33

Your fold should look like this. Do the same on the other side.

34

Unfold it and, as in step 31, you should have 3 crease lines.

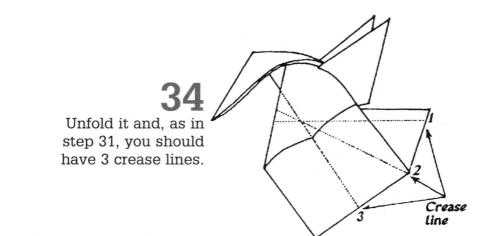

35

Push up Crease Line 2 and bring Crease Lines 1 & 3 together (the same way you would push up the tail).

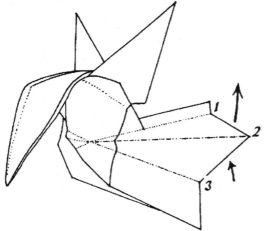

36

Your plane should look like this. Repeat Steps 34 & 35 on the other side.

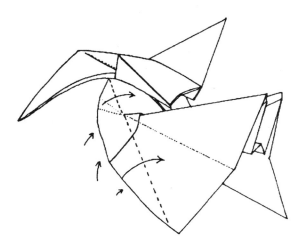

37

As you bring up the tail fin, the side shown here will collapse inward. Carefully fold it inward along the dotted line, as indicated by the arrows. Do the same to the other side.

38

Your plane should look exactly like this. Fold the stabilizers up. Make sure you duplicate this pattern on both sides.

39

Now, fold the stabilizers down. Do the same on the other side.

40

Open the stabilizers down completely.

41

Your plane should look like
this. Crease Lines V & W
should be visible.

42

Using the inward-up folding techniques you learned
when folding the jet's tail stabilizers and tail fins, fold
the tail inward and up on Crease Line V.

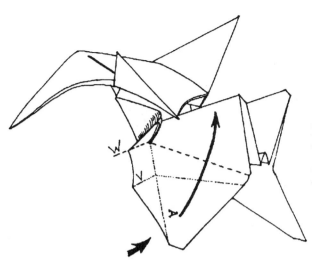

43

Fold Edge A inward-up on dotted Line W, as you did to make the tail fin.

44

Your plane should look like this. Fold the stabilizers down. Repeat on the other side.

45

Your plane should look like this.

Press hard together

Push

46

Press the body tightly together. Push down at the
tail joint to separate the two tails.

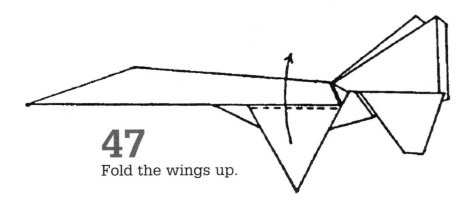

47

Fold the wings up.

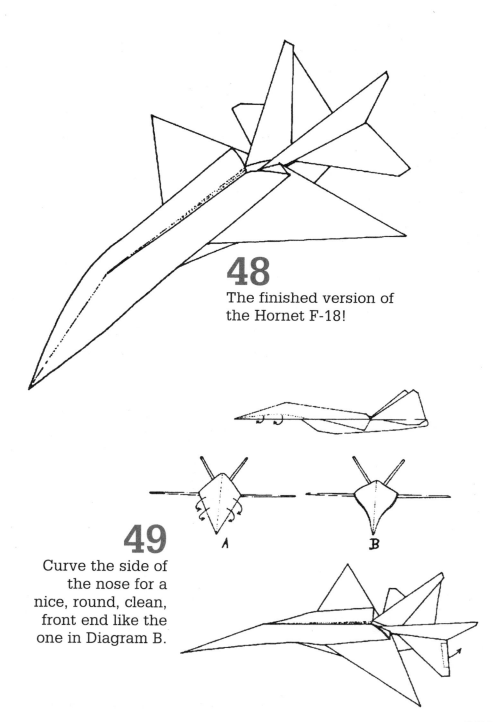

48

The finished version of
the Hornet F-18!

49

Curve the side of
the nose for a
nice, round, clean,
front end like the
one in Diagram B.

A

B

208

F-14 TOMCAT

You're about to receive your "Top Gun U.S. F-14 Tomcat Trophy" for achieving the pinnacle in the art of paper airmanship. This plane will dazzle your eyes. Its structure is that of a real F-14 Tomcat and it will emulate the Tomcat's performance as well. You can fly it or treasure it, but make sure this plane is symmetrical & sturdy. For practice you may use an 8½ x 11 sheet of typing paper, but if you want the Tomcat to perform, use a 12½ x 15 or larger sheet of thin but strong paper.

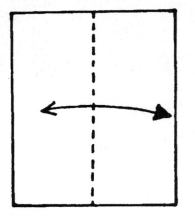

1

Fold paper in
half, then unfold.

2

Fold diagonally
at dotted lines,
then unfold.

3

Now, use both
hands and fold the
paper up and in
toward the middle.

4

This is how the
paper should look.
Gently press down
from the top.

5

Now, it should
look like this.

6

Slide your right hand
under Flap X as
shown here.

7

Flip Flap X over
and onto Flap A.

8

Flap X should line up
evenly with Flap A on
the left side.

9

Now, fold Flap X on
the dotted line
toward the centerline.

10

This is how your
fold should look.

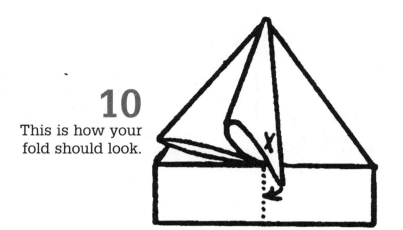

11

After you have folded
Flap X toward the middle
flap, flip it to the right
side. Notice Edge B.

12

This is how your plane
should look. Now,
unfold & flip the right
wing to the left side.

13

This is how it should look after you've flipped it to the left. Now fold on the dotted line so that Corner X meets Corner H.

14

This is how Step 13 should look. Repeat this fold on the left side.

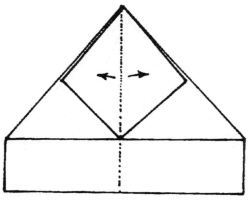

15

After you fold the left side, open both sides as indicated here.

16

Now open the wings further. The front wings now have two intersecting crease lines. Label them P and O.

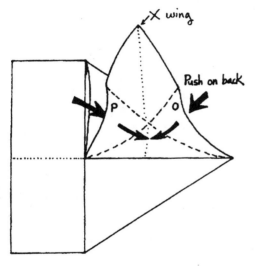

17

Rotate your paper ¼ turn to the right and fold P & O together and toward you on the crossing crease lines.

18

Your folds on P & O should look exactly as shown here. Put your hand behind the wing at M & N and press the two sides together.

NOTE: The fold here is similar to that used for the F-15 but it is shifted toward the M side instead of the N side.

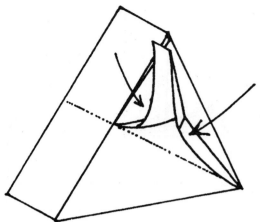

19

After pressing sides M & N together, this is how your plane should look. Do the same on the left side, beginning with Step 16, before going on.

20

Your finished folds of the wing should look like this. Fold the wing up toward the nose exactly as the arrow indicates.

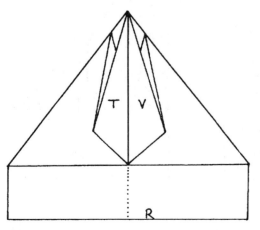

21

After you have finished with the other side, separate both sides as displayed. (Notice the R edge.)

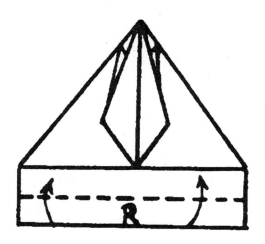

22

Fold up the R edge
at the midpoint,
along the dotted line.

23

Now, fold back along
the dotted line.

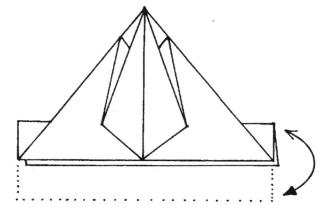

24

This is how your fold
toward the back
should look. Now
unfold it as shown, so
that it looks like the
end of step 22.

25

Fold diagonally up, then back and forth at each corner, as shown here.

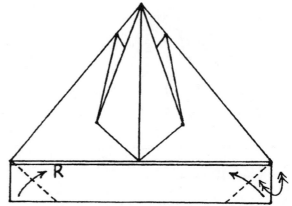

26

This is how the folds on step 25 should look. Fold back and forth five or six times.

27

After you've folded the corners, unfold the R edge fold as shown. You should have two triangular shapes.

28

Push the two triangular
sides inward as shown.

29

After you have pressed
both triangular sides
inward, it should look
like this. Now, fold this
part back on the dotted
line. Next, flip the V
wing to the T wing on
the left side.

30

Now, fold Edge B to
Centerline C on the
dotted line. Do the
same to the left side.

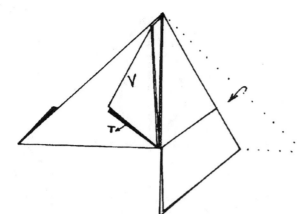

31

Fold Wing V to the left. Now your plane should look like this.

32

Fold Wing V down as shown here and align with the fuselage.

2³/⁴ "

3"

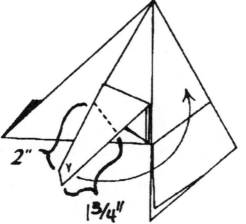

2"

1³/⁴"

33

Your fold should look exactly like this. Now fold up toward the right. Remember to make crisp folds.

34

Your fold should look exactly like this. Now fold straight to the left.

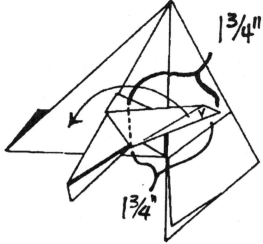

35

Your V wing should look like this. Make an even-opposite fold, following Steps 32-35, on the other side.

36

When the left side is finished, separate the sides and your plane should look like this. Look at the wings carefully now. You will be tucking the wings next but they will have this same definite appearance when finished.

NOTE: the purpose of this tuck is to make the wings more rigid and sturdy.

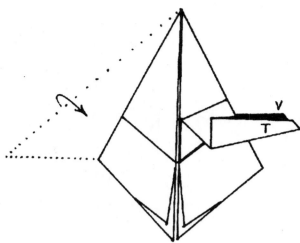

37

Flip the left Wing T over to the right and fold the left side to the middle. Your plane should look like this.

38

Unfold both wings, flip Wing V to the left and the plane should look like this. Crease Lines 1, 2 & 3 should be visible.

NOTE: You must know or mark the 3 crease lines.

39

Very carefully open Wing V & fold down on Crease Line 2. (Simply tuck in the wing, downward, along dotted Crease Line 2.)

40

Fold it back up on Crease Line 3. Make sure Crease Line 3 is tucked in between Creases 1 & 2 exactly as shown here. Close the wing's side together so it looks like Step 36.

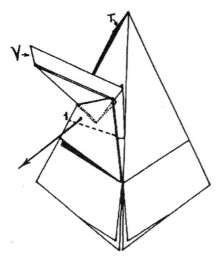

41

Your wing fold should look like this. Fold down on Crease Line 1.

42

Your plane should look like this. Carefully repeat Steps 39–41 on left Wing T.

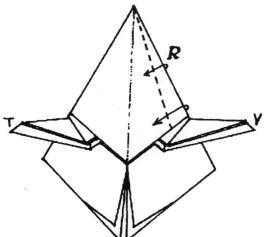

43

Finish the left side and separate the wings; your plane should look like this. Fold Edge R halfway to the center along the dotted line.

44

As you fold, put your finger in the pocket where the arrow is pointing. Roll your finger toward the center of the fuselage. Flatten the small triangle.

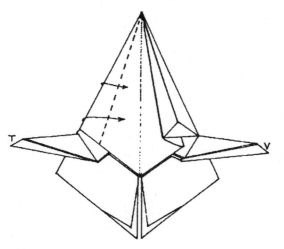

45

Your plane should look like this. Do the same on the left side.

46

Turn the model over and your plane should look like this.

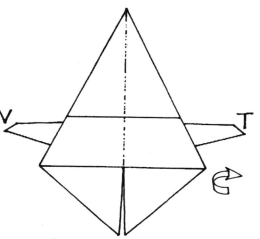

47

Fold the right side to the middle along the dotted line.

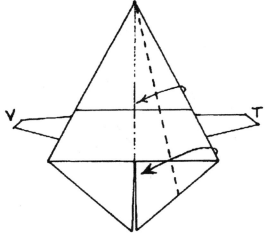

48

Your fold should look like this. Do the same on the left side.

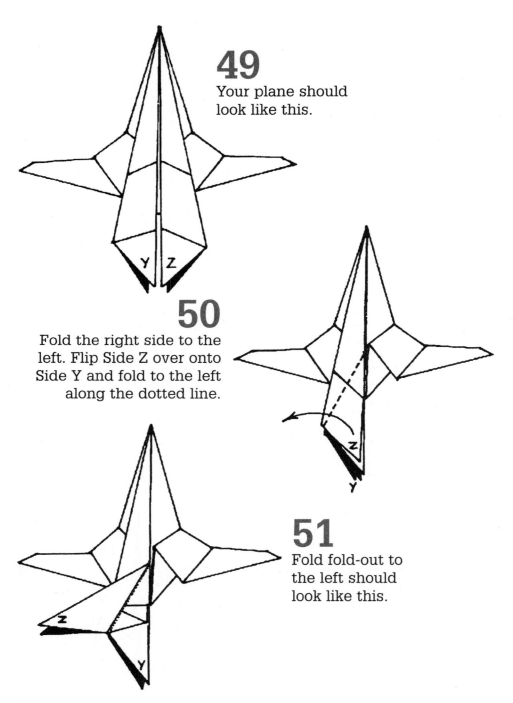

49

Your plane should
look like this.

50

Fold the right side to the
left. Flip Side Z over onto
Side Y and fold to the left
along the dotted line.

51

Fold fold-out to
the left should
look like this.

52

Flip Side Z back to the right.
Do the same on the left side.

53

Turn the plane over
and it should look
like this.

54

Unfold the right side
stabilizer and the tail fin.

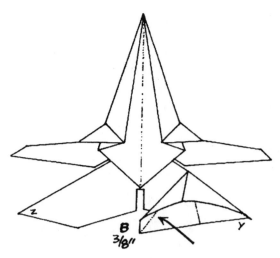

55

Put your finger in the pocket indicated by the arrow. Slowly move your finger upward, creating Edge S.

56

Your fold should now look exactly like this. Fold Stabilizer B toward Tail Fin Y on the dotted line.

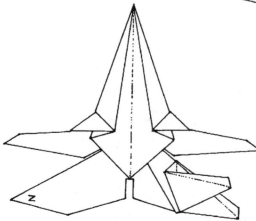

57

The fold to the right should look like this. Do the same on the left side.

58

Your tail folds should look like this.

59

Now fold the nose down and align the back as you did on the F-15. Then fold the tail up. Next, put your finger in the pocket indicated by the big arrow and pull out for the engine.

60
The finished version
of the F-14 Tomcat!

61
Put some tape in
the spots shown
here and your
plane will be ready
to fly. Throw the
plane straight out
from your body and
it will fly smoothly.

Tape

Tape

F-86 SABRE

The F-86 uses more advanced folds than even the F-14 and it is recommended that you complete the other models before folding this plane.

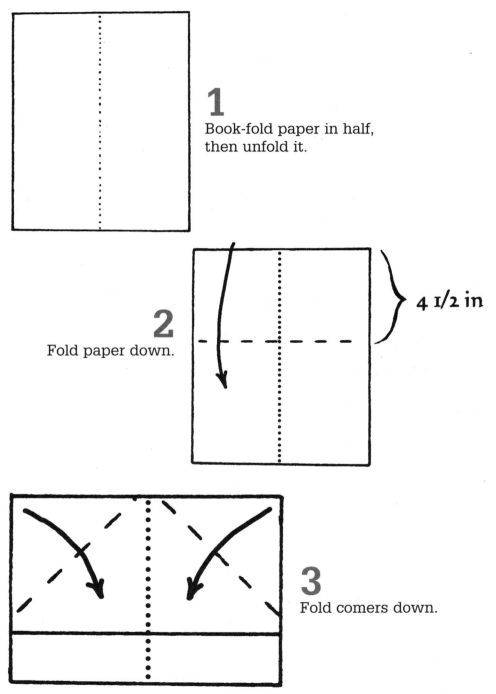

1
Book-fold paper in half,
then unfold it.

2
Fold paper down.

4 1/2 in

3
Fold comers down.

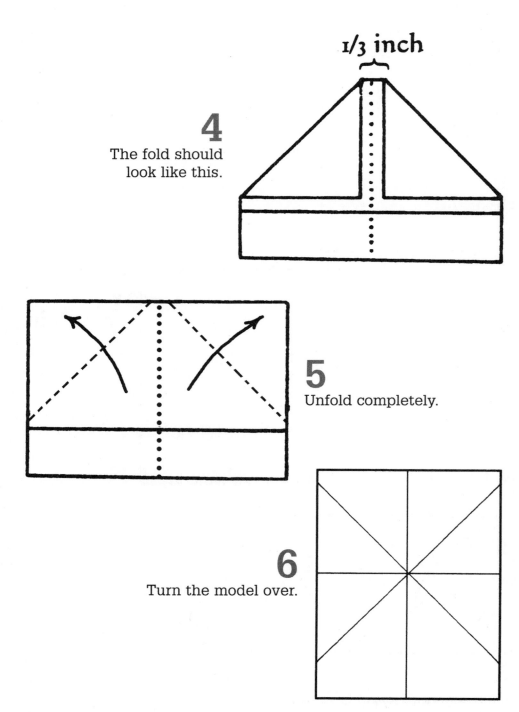

1/3 inch

4

The fold should
look like this.

5

Unfold completely.

6

Turn the model over.

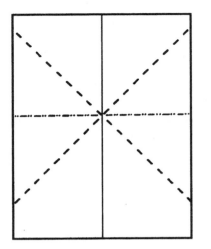

7

Press the center point with your finger, and the paper will fold upwards.

8

This is the folding diagram for the base. Fold the sides in and the top down.

flat top toward you

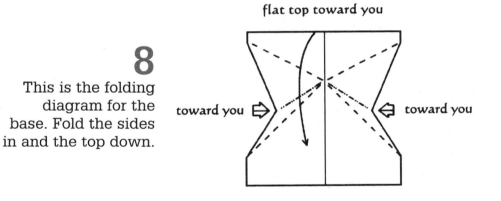

toward you ⇨   ⇦ toward you

9

Base completed.

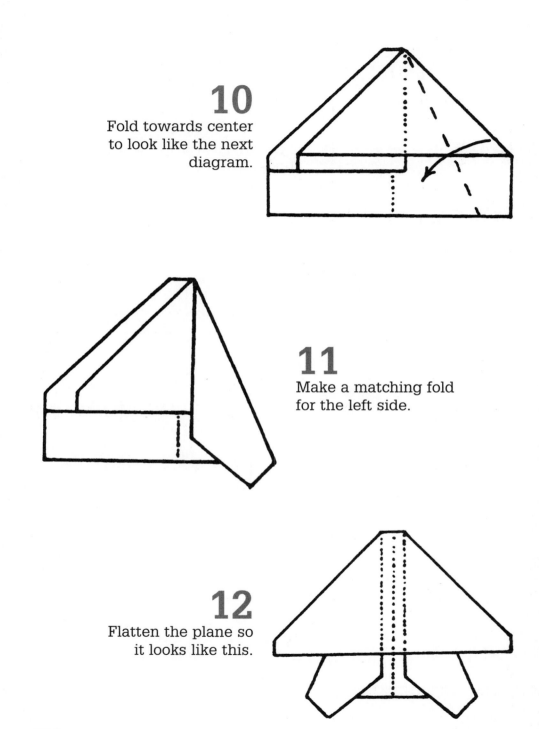

10
Fold towards center to look like the next diagram.

11
Make a matching fold for the left side.

12
Flatten the plane so it looks like this.

13

Cut or tear on dashed line to look like the next step.

14

Fold edge up.

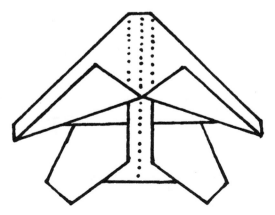

15

Reverse this fold to the inside.

16
Completion of fold
to the inside.

17
Fold edge to right side to
look like the next step.

18
Make a matching fold
for the left side.

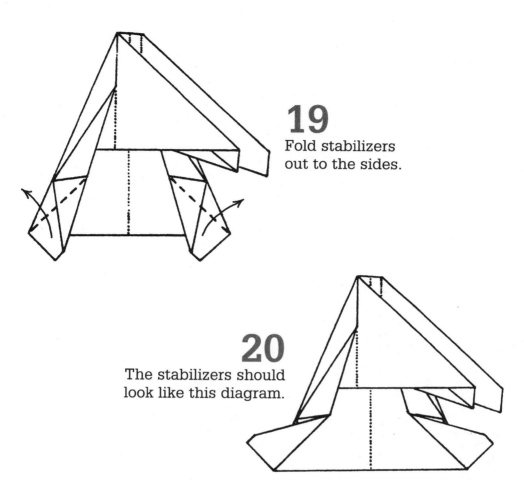

19
Fold stabilizers
out to the sides.

20
The stabilizers should
look like this diagram.

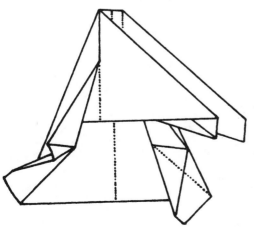

21
Unfold stabilizers
back down and make
an inside reverse
fold out again.

22

Completion of inside-reverse fold for the stabilizers. Book-fold flap across center.

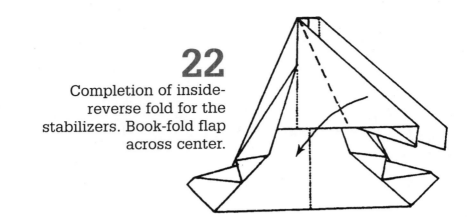

23

Fold flap up on dashed line.

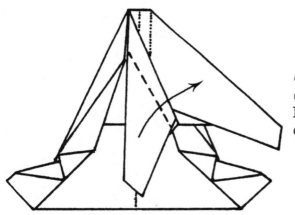

24

The wing folds out like this diagram. Make a matching fold for the right side.

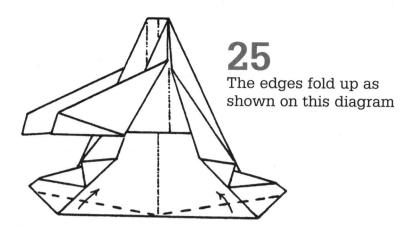

25

The edges fold up as shown on this diagram

26

Both edges should look like the right side of this diagram.

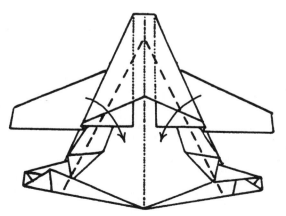

27

Insert right stabilizer under the flap that had been behind it. Do same to the left side. Make the fuselage fold.

28

Completion of fuselage fold. Fold wings and stabilizers up.

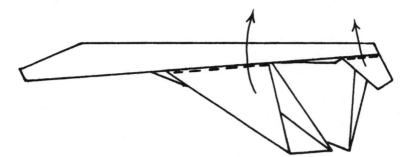

29

To create the tail, do an inside-reverse fold: fold the belly of the plane up between the wings to get a pointed tail, then fold the top of the tail back down into itself to give the tail its correct shape. (See Inside-Reverse Fold in the front of the book if you need help.)

30
Completed F-86 Sabre!

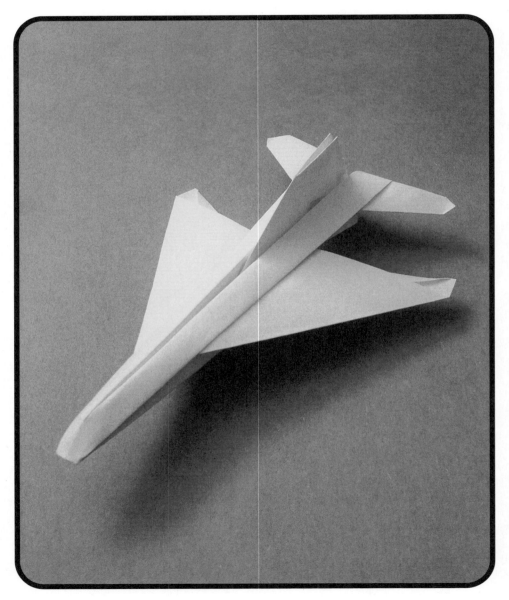

BONUS SECTION

mini *Paper Planes*

Small but Extraordinary Paper Planes You Can Make!

Michael Weinstein

Symbols

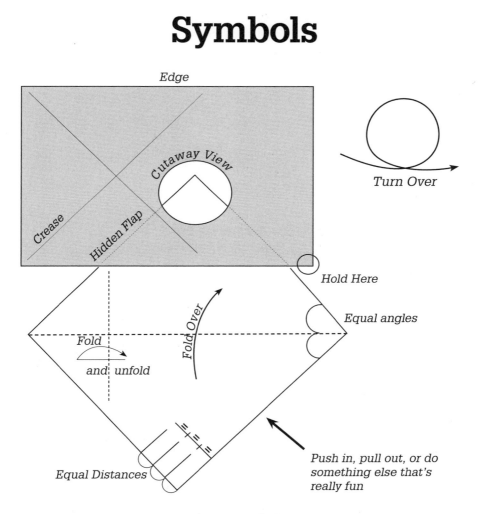

Edge

Cutaway View

Crease

Hidden Flap

Turn Over

Hold Here

Equal angles

Fold Over

Fold

and unfold

Equal Distances

Push in, pull out, or do something else that's really fun

Valley fold

Fold so the crease points away from you (and the flap toward you).

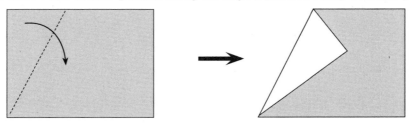

Mountain fold
Fold so that the crease points toward you (and the flap away from you).

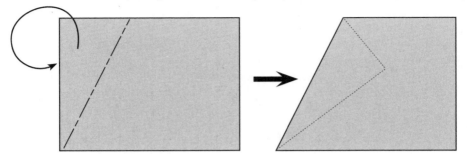

Inside Reverse fold
Fold so that a point falls between layers.

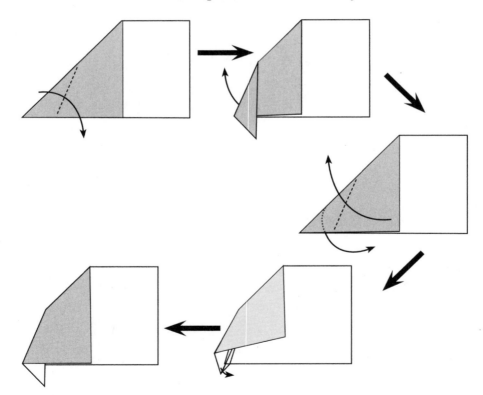

Outside Reverse fold
Fold so that a point wraps around the outside of two layers.

Rabbit Ear
Pull out a hidden layer and fold it flat.

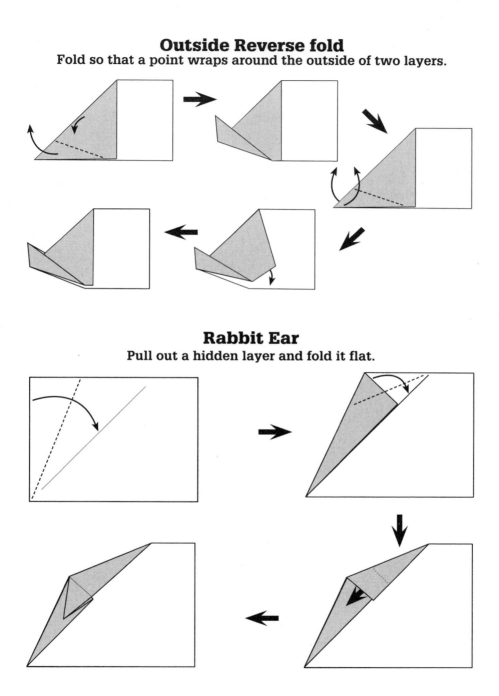

Squash fold
Separate two adjacent layers and flatten the pocket
that forms between them.

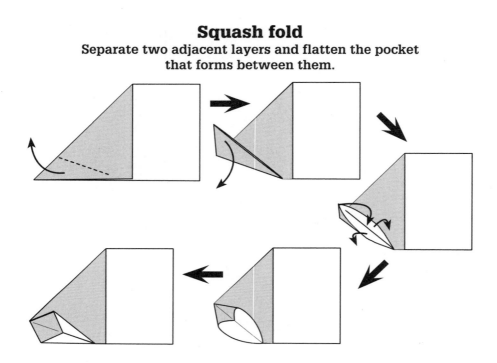

Petal fold
Separate two layers while flattening the pockets that form on either side.

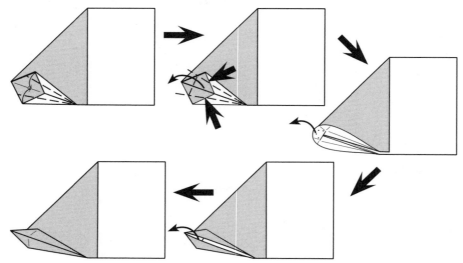

Sink fold

A multi-layered point gets pushed to the inside. The point is partially
unfolded and mountain folded at the desired position.

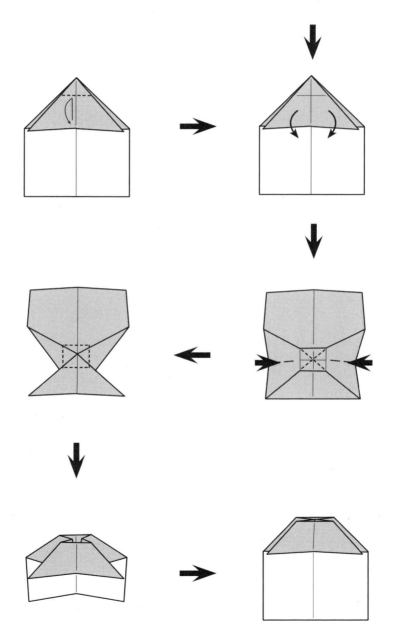

Paper Airplane Bases

Origami models often involve the same steps at the beginning. For example, if you wanted to fold a bird, you would need a head, neck, tail, and wings. In fact, one of the classic origami bases is the bird base, from which these structures are easily derived. The origami genius John Montrol has developed a dog base, from which one can readily fold the parts needed for a four-footed animal. Many of the airplanes in this book are derived from a set of common precursors, instructions for which follow on the next page. The Airplane Base is short, and generates two evenly sized sets of wings. The Canard Base is the basis for most of the canard, or forward-wing aircraft.

Airplane Base

This will make two sets of wings, or one set of wings and one set of...

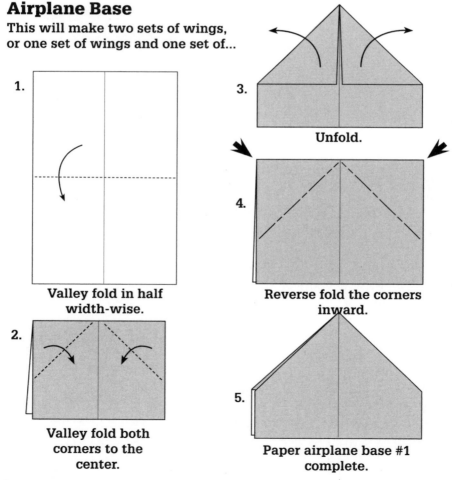

1.

Valley fold in half width-wise.

2.

Valley fold both corners to the center.

3.

Unfold.

4.

Reverse fold the corners inward.

5.

Paper airplane base #1 complete.

Canard Base

This base makes it easy to design canard, or forward-wing aircraft, because it generates two flaps in the front that can easily be manipulated to make many shapes and do a number of interesting things.

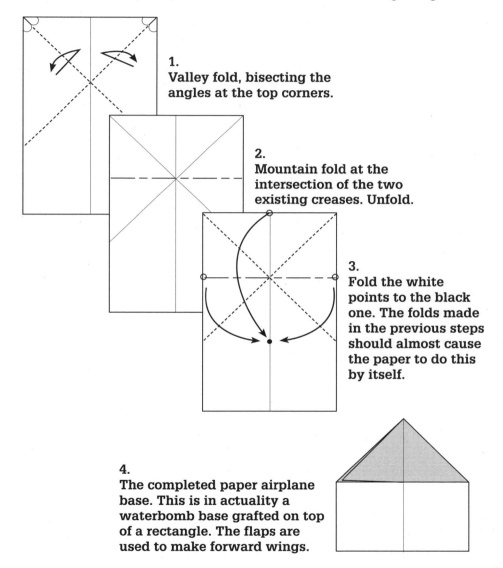

1.
Valley fold, bisecting the angles at the top corners.

2.
Mountain fold at the intersection of the two existing creases. Unfold.

3.
Fold the white points to the black one. The folds made in the previous steps should almost cause the paper to do this by itself.

4.
The completed paper airplane base. This is in actuality a waterbomb base grafted on top of a rectangle. The flaps are used to make forward wings.

Making and flying paper airplanes is educational, recreational, environmental (all that recycling of paper) and just plain fun. There are, of course, a few things that aid in the pursuit of the perfect plane.

Paper

Many kinds of paper are good for the aspiring parchment pilot. All of them are reasonably thick and strong; newspaper makes lousy fighter bombers, for instance. On the other hand, too much thickness spoils the party. Posterboard makes for really tough Origami, and most reasonably cool paper airplanes wouldn't dream of being made from construction paper. The paper must also hold a crease fairly well, so most softer papers are way out of it. Copier paper is one of my favorites, as it combines strength, light weight, and durability.

Amost all of the airplanes here are made from paper that is 8½ × 5½ inches (A5-size). This is not some mysterious paper only available in the finer bookstores of Tibet, but is a half sheet of ordinary 8½ × 11 inch (A-4 size) paper, available everywhere. When creating my cellulose squadron I noticed that a normal-sized piece of paper was sort of short and didn't leave me much room to play around and do fun and interesting things (like use a Pagoda to create Canard wings). I found that a half-sheet was longer, and more fun to create with.

The craft contained within are all indoor flyers (growing up in northern Ohio, we had to appreciate good-weather days, all two of them). Being manufactured from smaller paper makes them lighter and more nimble than their larger brethren. Making the required size of paper is very simple; fold an 8½ × 11 (A4-size) piece of paper in half, and cut along the crease. A paper-cutter makes it even easier. If you're locked in a room with none of these things, you can simply tear a piece of paper in half.

How to Make an 8½ × 5½ Inch (A5-size) Sheet of Paper

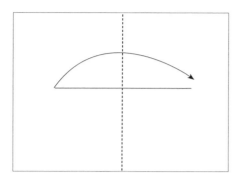

Fold an 8½ × 11 inch (A4-size) sheet of paper in half, and crease really well. Unfold.

Hold the paper so the crease faces up toward you. Pull evenly around the crease at the part nearest to you.

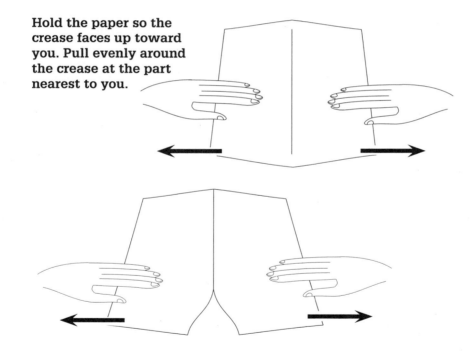

The paper should start to tear where the midline crease meets the forward edge. Continue to apply pressure evenly, and the paper will tear very neatly in half. With a bit of practice, this becomes really easy, and faster than scissors!

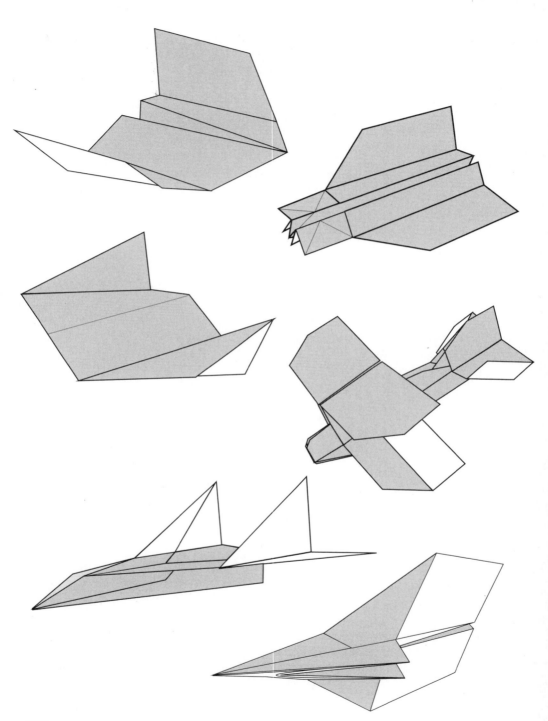

THE PLANES

Have fun and happy landings!

THIRDSIES

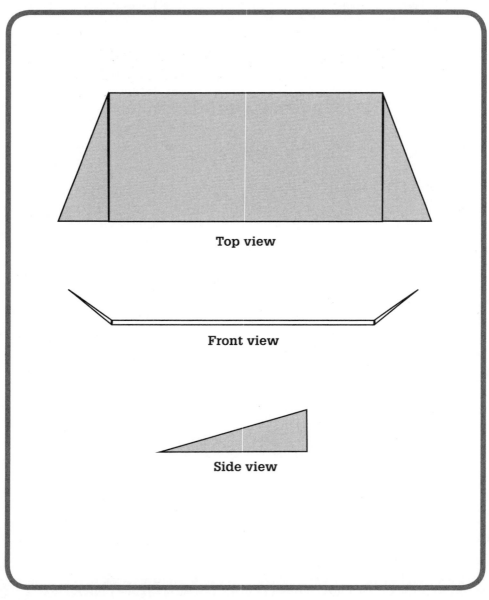

Top view

Front view

Side view

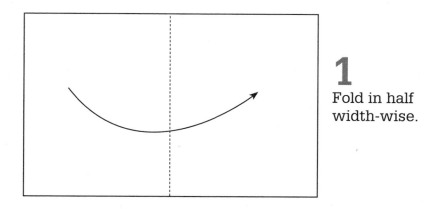

1

Fold in half
width-wise.

2

Unfold.

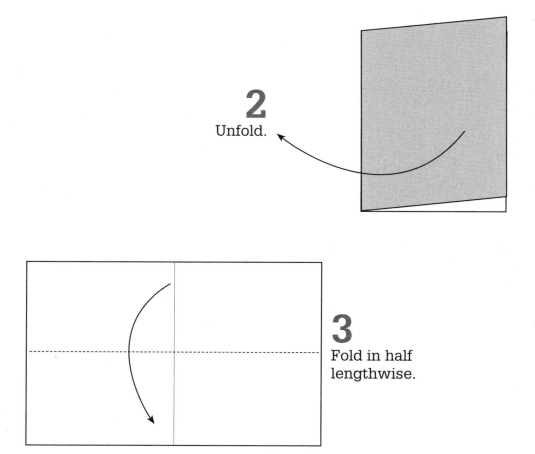

3

Fold in half
lengthwise.

4
Unfold.

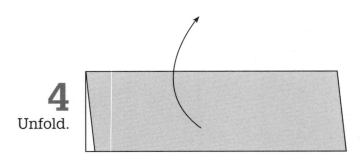

5
Fold so that the top corner lies along the crease made in Step 3.

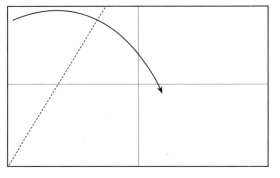

6
Like so. Unfold, and repeat on the other side.

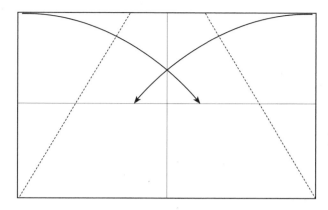

7

Fold the corners in along the creases made earlier. One will lie on top of the other.

8

Valley fold the top down so that the top edge lies on the corners.

9

Unfold.

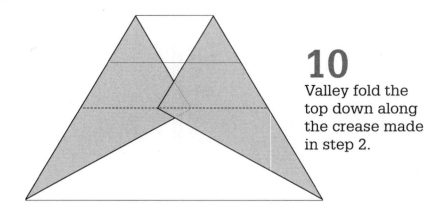

10

Valley fold the
top down along
the crease made
in step 2.

11

Mountain fold the
top all the way
underneath.

12

Fold back
the vertical
stabilizers.

THIRDSIES

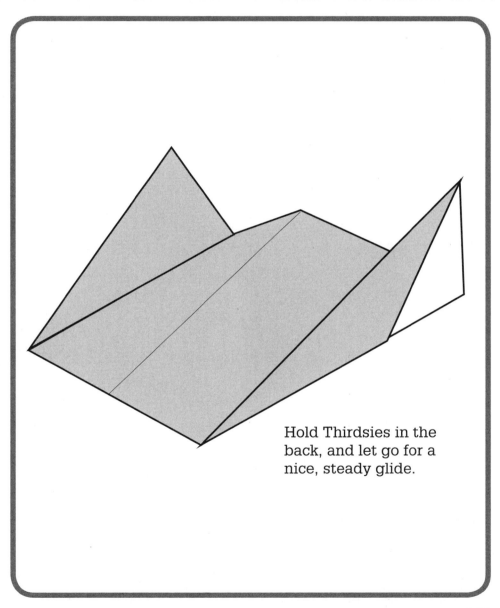

Hold Thirdsies in the back, and let go for a nice, steady glide.

BOTTLENOSE

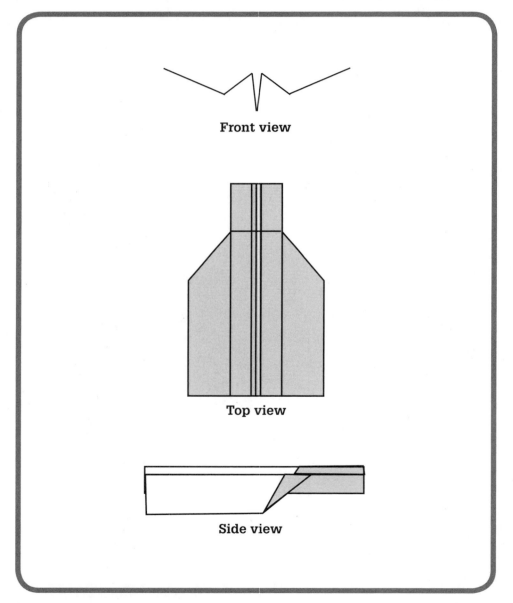

Front view

Top view

Side view

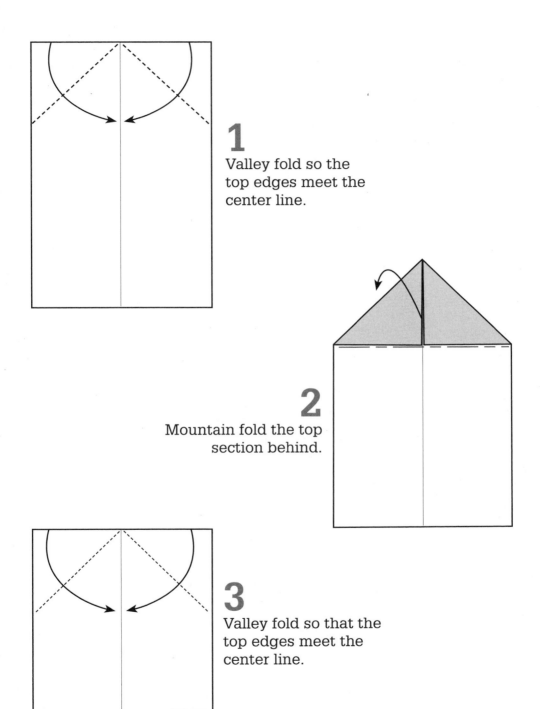

1
Valley fold so the top edges meet the center line.

2
Mountain fold the top section behind.

3
Valley fold so that the top edges meet the center line.

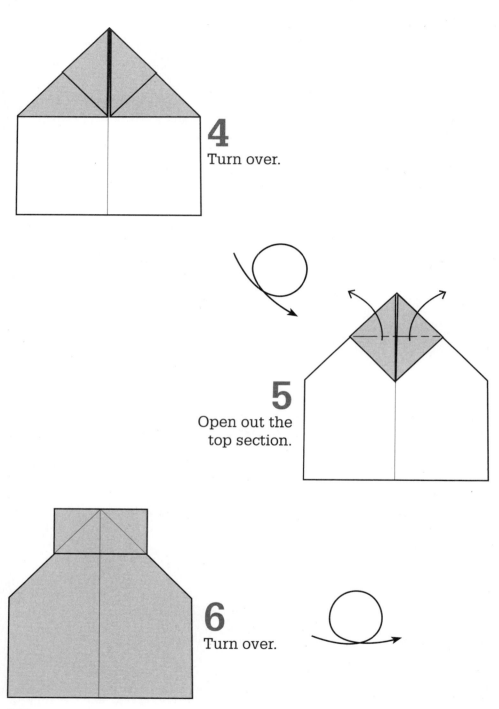

4
Turn over.

5
Open out the
top section.

6
Turn over.

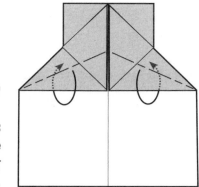

7

Mountain fold the flaps
underneath to thicken the
leading edges of the wing
and move weight forward.

8

Mountain fold the model
in half lengthwise.

9

Valley fold the wings
down by folding halfway
across the top.

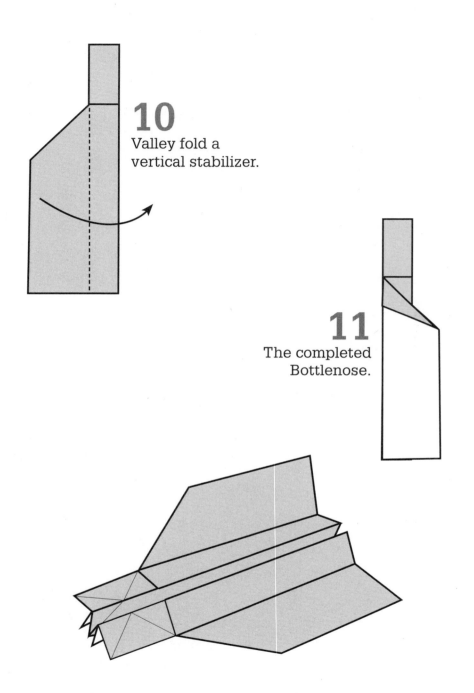

10
Valley fold a
vertical stabilizer.

11
The completed
Bottlenose.

RAPTOR

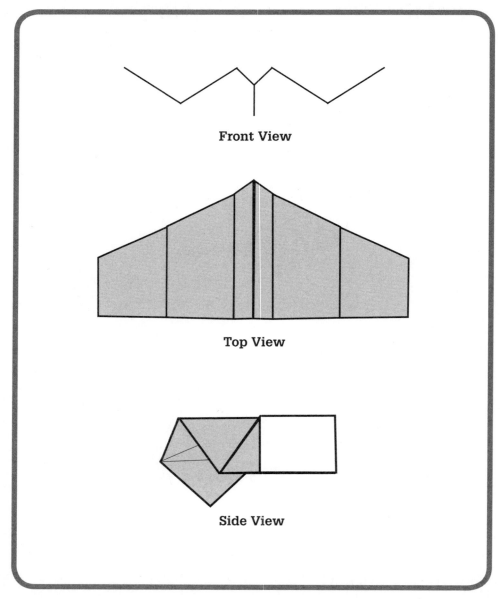

Front View

Top View

Side View

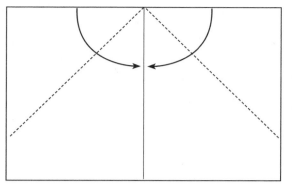

1
Valley fold the
top edges into the
center line.

2
Valley fold the top
edge down to the
raw edge below.

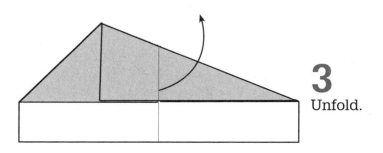

3
Unfold.

4

Repeat steps 2 and 3
on the other side.

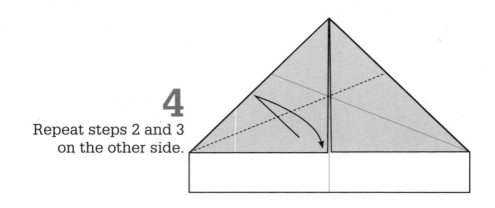

5

Valley fold the top
point down to meet the
intersection of the two
diagonal creases.

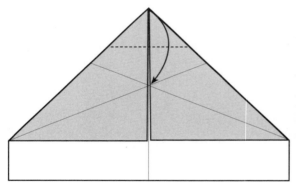

6

Rabbit ear the top
down and to the side.

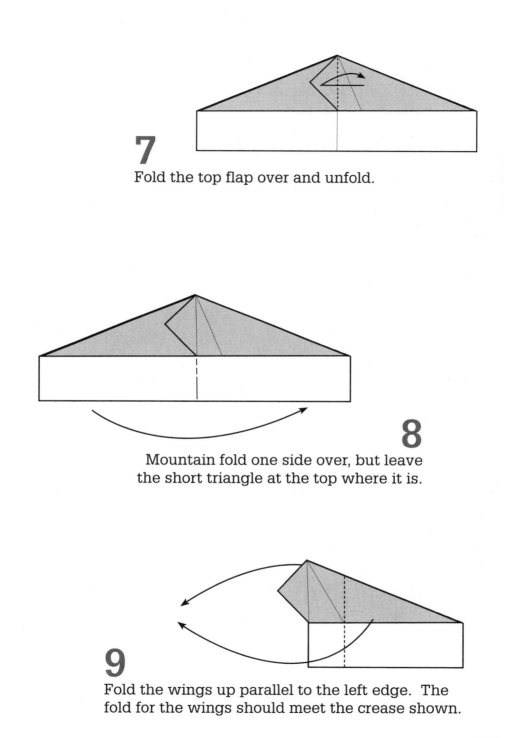

7

Fold the top flap over and unfold.

8

Mountain fold one side over, but leave the short triangle at the top where it is.

9

Fold the wings up parallel to the left edge. The fold for the wings should meet the crease shown.

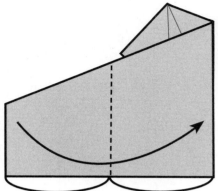

10

Fold the stabilizers up halfway down the wings.

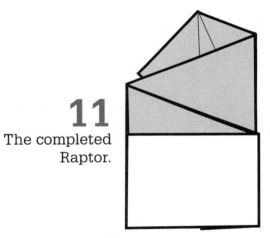

11

The completed Raptor.

SKEETER

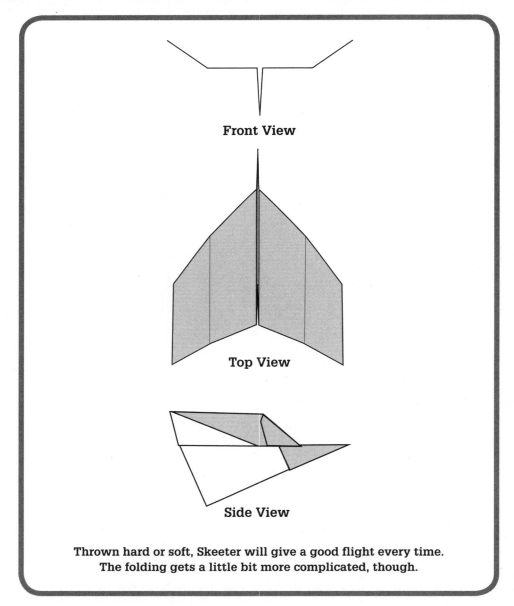

Front View

Top View

Side View

Thrown hard or soft, Skeeter will give a good flight every time.
The folding gets a little bit more complicated, though.

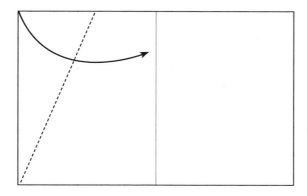

1

Valley fold so that the top corner lies on the center line. The fold should pass right through the bottom corner.

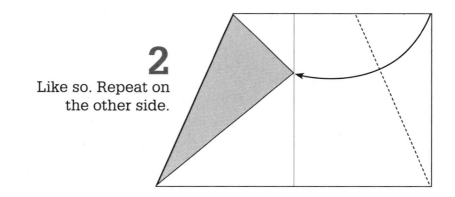

2

Like so. Repeat on the other side.

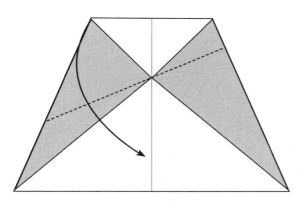

3

This gets a bit tricky. Valley fold so that the top left corner lies on the center line. Make sure that the fold runs through the intersection of the two flaps you just folded in.

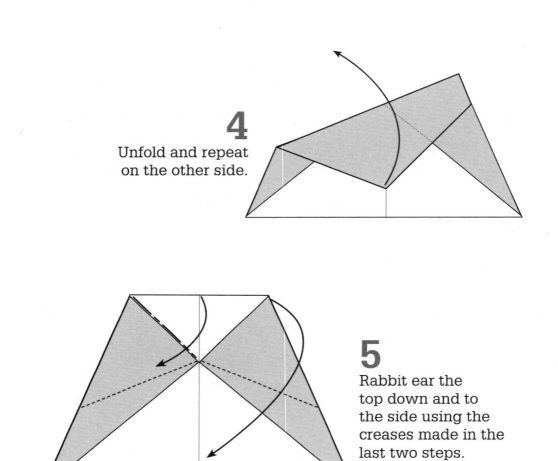

4
Unfold and repeat
on the other side.

5
Rabbit ear the
top down and to
the side using the
creases made in the
last two steps.

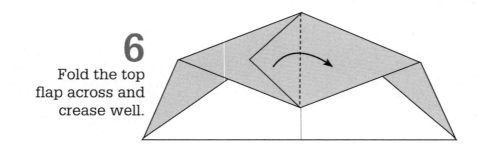

6
Fold the top
flap across and
crease well.

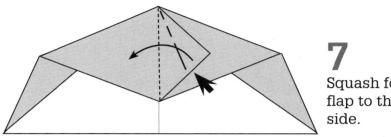

7

Squash fold the flap to the other side.

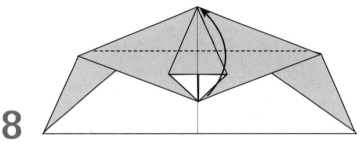

8

Valley fold the bottom point of the top layer (it consists of paired white flaps) to the topmost point. Carefully fold through all the layers.

9

Unfold.

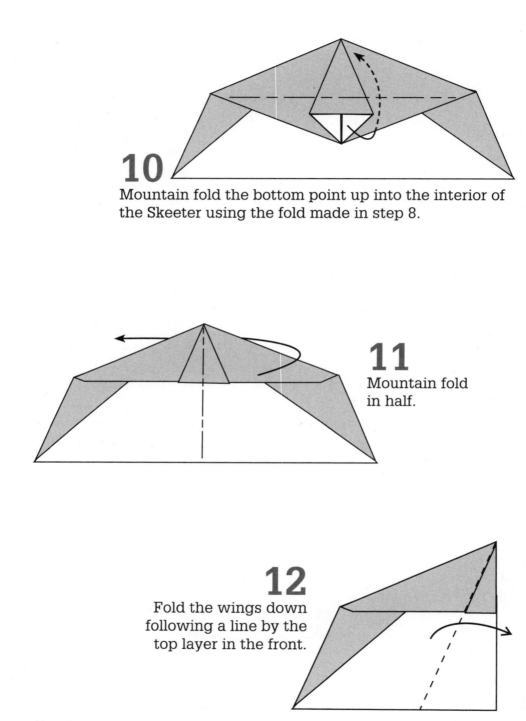

10
Mountain fold the bottom point up into the interior of
the Skeeter using the fold made in step 8.

11
Mountain fold
in half.

12
Fold the wings down
following a line by the
top layer in the front.

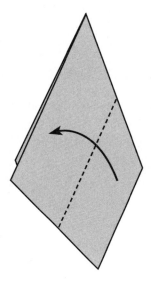

13

Fold vertical stabilizers
by bringing the outside
edge of the wings to meet
the inside edge.

14

The completed
Skeeter.

GLIDER SUPREME

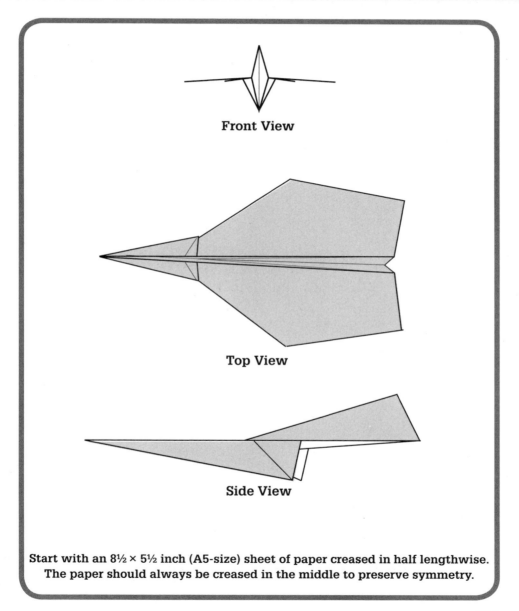

Front View

Top View

Side View

Start with an 8½ × 5½ inch (A5-size) sheet of paper creased in half lengthwise. The paper should always be creased in the middle to preserve symmetry.

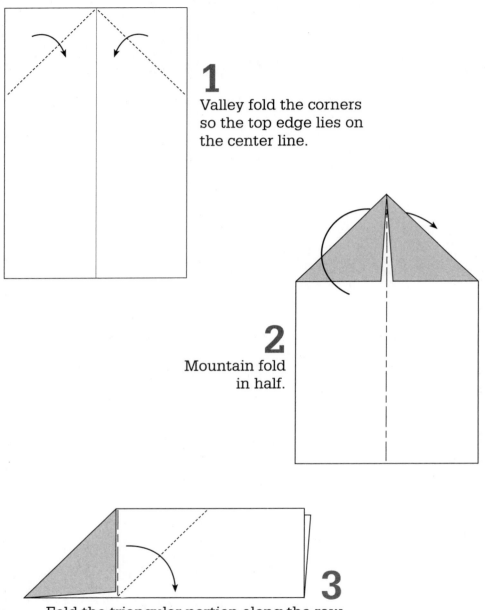

1
Valley fold the corners so the top edge lies on the center line.

2
Mountain fold in half.

3
Fold the triangular portion along the raw edge. The mountain fold should line up with the folded edge at the bottom.

4

Outside reverse
fold the triangle
in front.

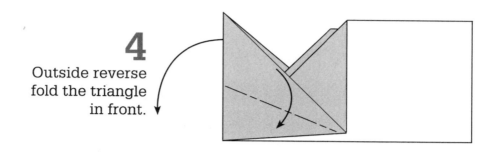

5

Open the model
and flatten out the
forward portion.

6

Valley fold
in half.

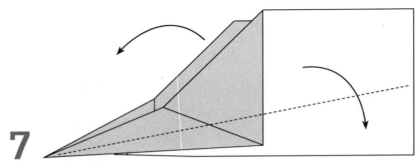

7

Bisecting the angle in front,
Valley fold the wings.

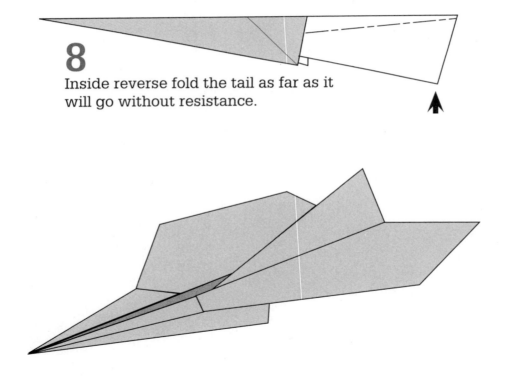

8

Inside reverse fold the tail as far as it
will go without resistance.

GLIDER SUPREME

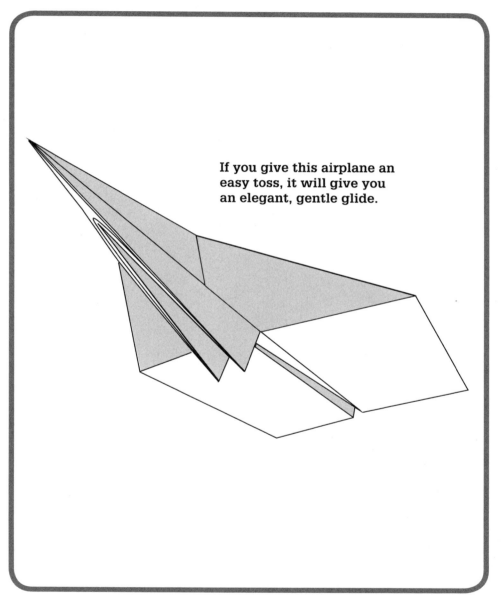

If you give this airplane an easy toss, it will give you an elegant, gentle glide.

ELAPSE

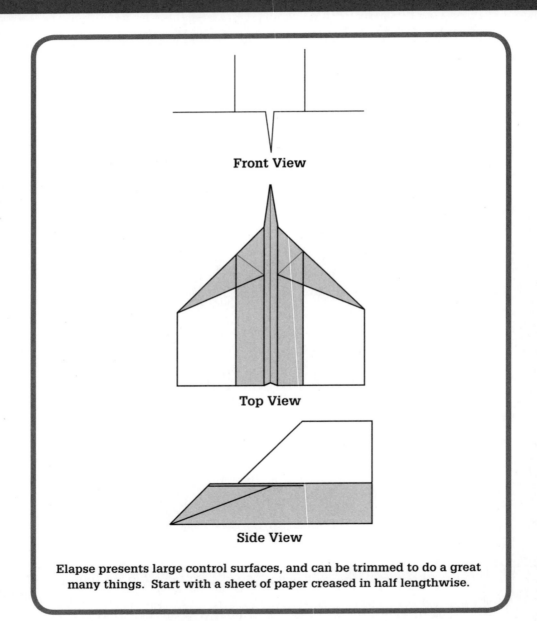

Front View

Top View

Side View

Elapse presents large control surfaces, and can be trimmed to do a great many things. Start with a sheet of paper creased in half lengthwise.

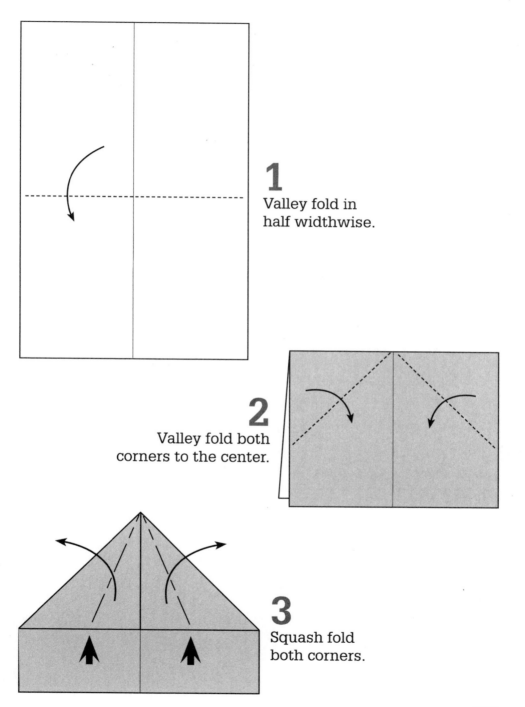

1 Valley fold in half widthwise.

2 Valley fold both corners to the center.

3 Squash fold both corners.

4

Petal fold on both sides.

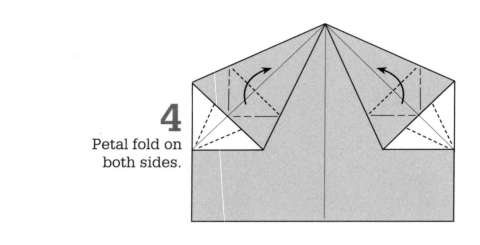

5

Mountain fold the half diamonds behind.

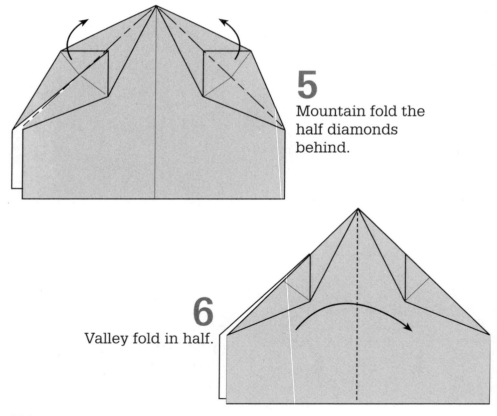

6

Valley fold in half.

7

Valley fold the wings
down.

8

Valley fold one layer only on
the front and the back for
stabilizers.

9

Elapse complete.

F-14 TOMCAT

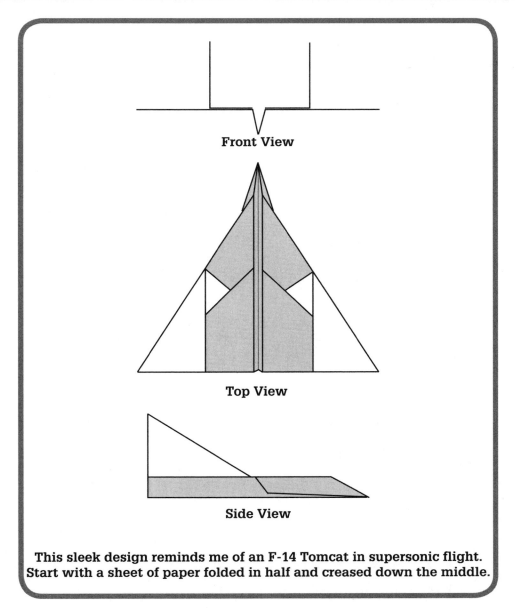

Front View

Top View

Side View

This sleek design reminds me of an F-14 Tomcat in supersonic flight.
Start with a sheet of paper folded in half and creased down the middle.

293

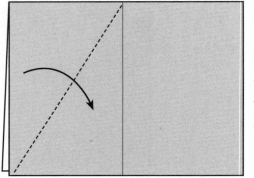

1
Valley fold from
top center to
bottom corner.

2
Squash fold the
resulting flap.

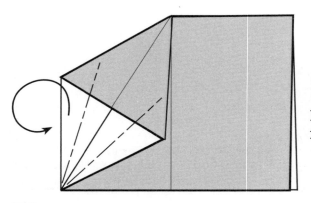

3
Mountain fold the
flaps in half.

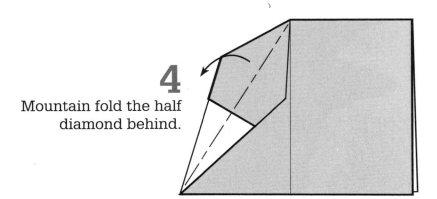

4

Mountain fold the half
diamond behind.

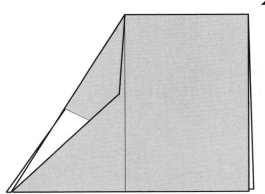

5

Repeat steps 1-4
on the other side.

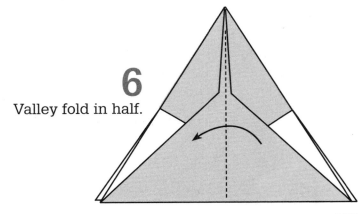

6

Valley fold in half.

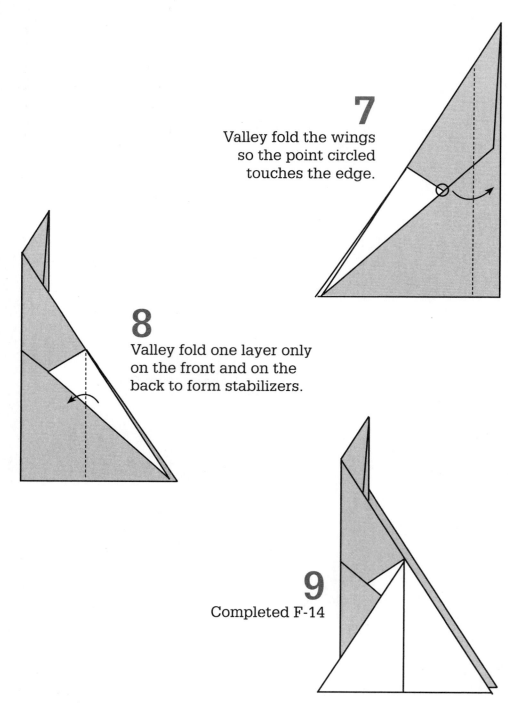

7

Valley fold the wings
so the point circled
touches the edge.

8

Valley fold one layer only
on the front and on the
back to form stabilizers.

9

Completed F-14

F-14 TOMCAT

OMEGA FLYER

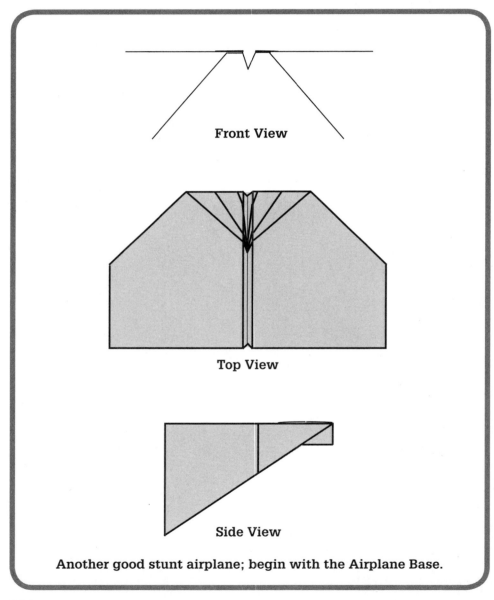

Front View

Top View

Side View

Another good stunt airplane; begin with the Airplane Base.

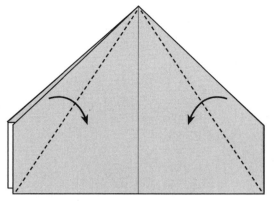

1

Valley fold from the top point to the lower corner on the top layer only.

2

Mountain fold the top so the point touches the base of the upper triangular area.

3

Mountain fold in half.

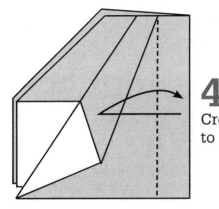

4

Crease the outside flaps to form stabilizers.

5

And valley fold the wings.

OMEGA FLYER

LOOPMAKER

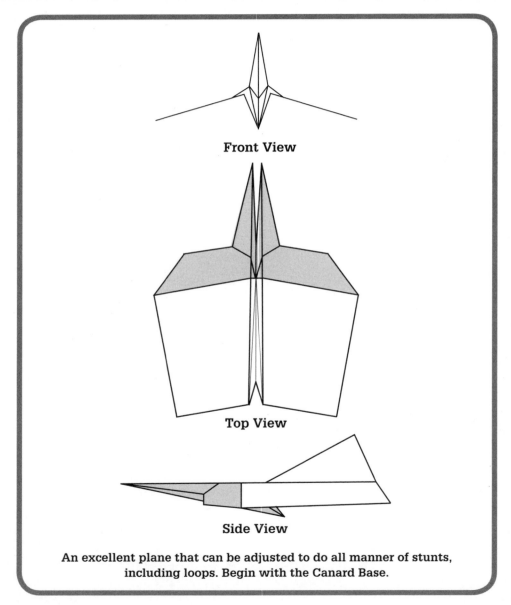

Front View

Top View

Side View

An excellent plane that can be adjusted to do all manner of stunts, including loops. Begin with the Canard Base.

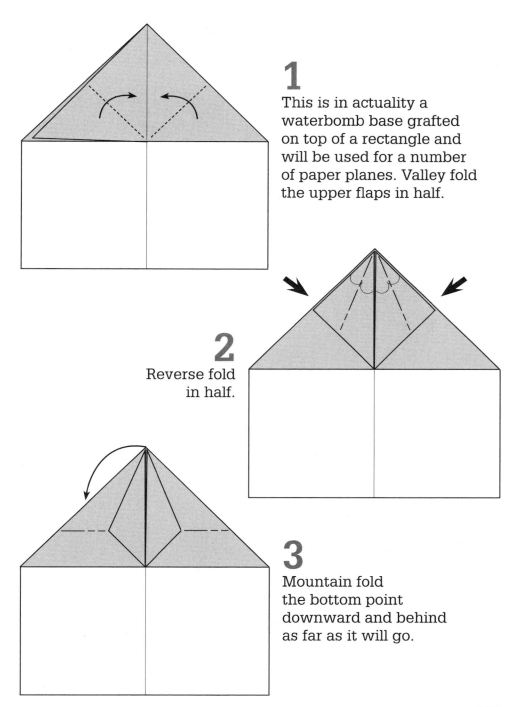

1

This is in actuality a waterbomb base grafted on top of a rectangle and will be used for a number of paper planes. Valley fold the upper flaps in half.

2

Reverse fold in half.

3

Mountain fold the bottom point downward and behind as far as it will go.

303

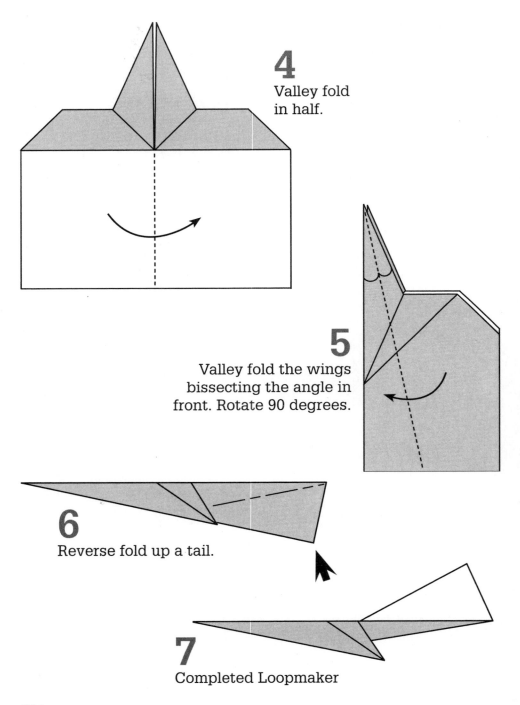

4
Valley fold
in half.

5
Valley fold the wings
bissecting the angle in
front. Rotate 90 degrees.

6
Reverse fold up a tail.

7
Completed Loopmaker

LOOPMAKER

MACH II

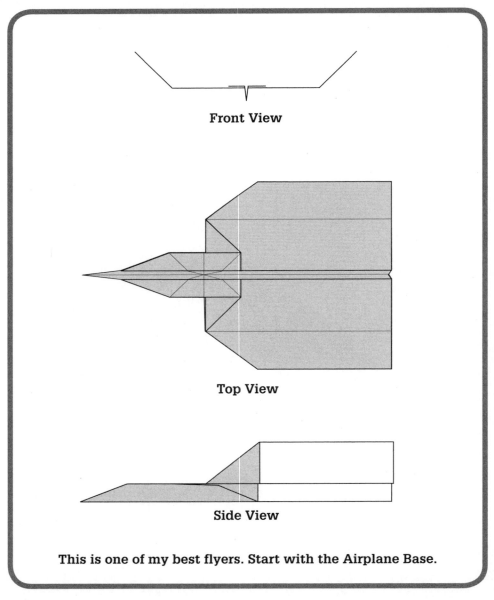

Front View

Top View

Side View

This is one of my best flyers. Start with the Airplane Base.

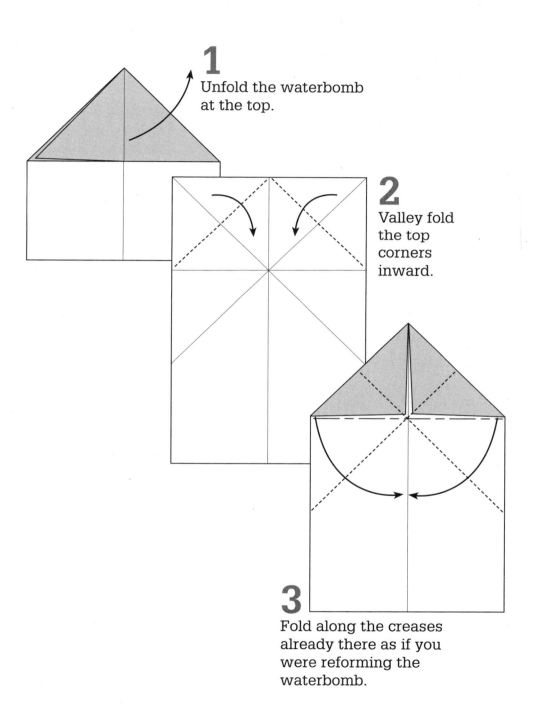

1
Unfold the waterbomb at the top.

2
Valley fold the top corners inward.

3
Fold along the creases already there as if you were reforming the waterbomb.

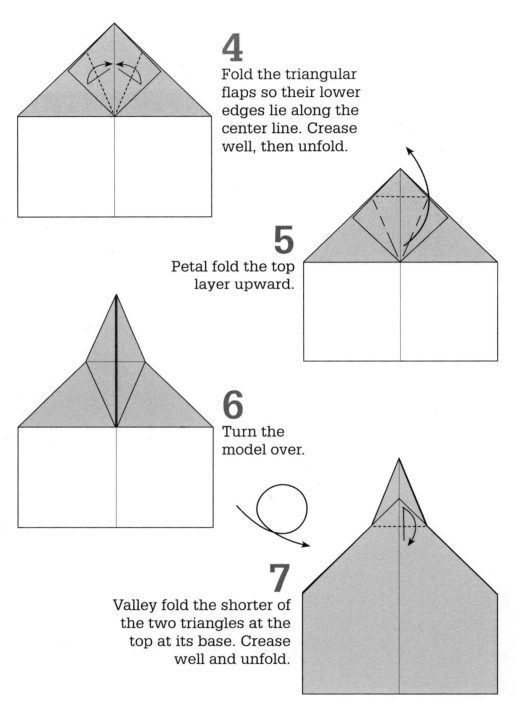

4

Fold the triangular flaps so their lower edges lie along the center line. Crease well, then unfold.

5

Petal fold the top layer upward.

6

Turn the model over.

7

Valley fold the shorter of the two triangles at the top at its base. Crease well and unfold.

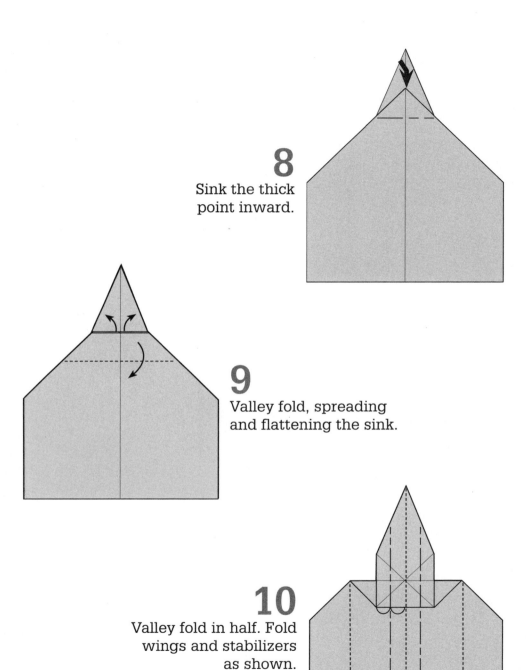

8

Sink the thick
point inward.

9

Valley fold, spreading
and flattening the sink.

10

Valley fold in half. Fold
wings and stabilizers
as shown.

MACH II

MULTI-STAGE CRAFT

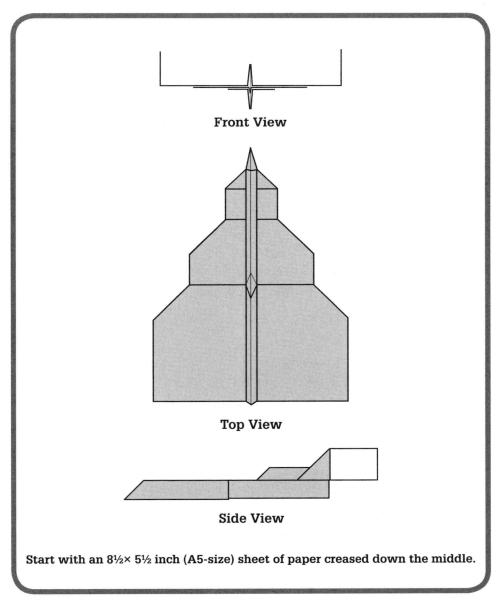

Front View

Top View

Side View

Start with an 8½× 5½ inch (A5-size) sheet of paper creased down the middle.

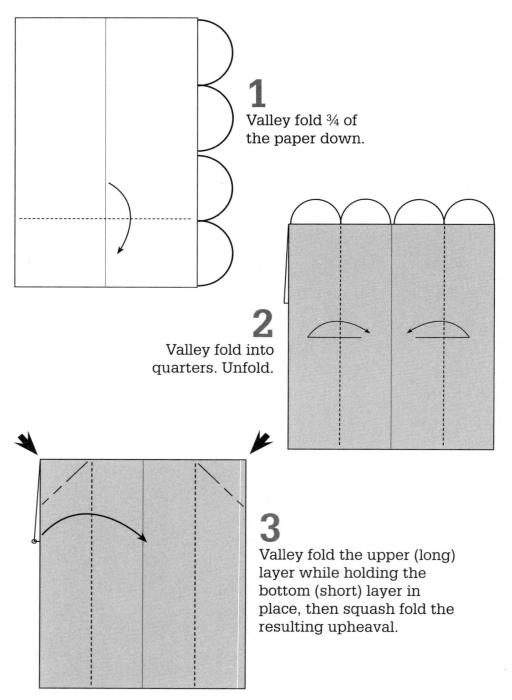

1

Valley fold ¾ of
the paper down.

2

Valley fold into
quarters. Unfold.

3

Valley fold the upper (long)
layer while holding the
bottom (short) layer in
place, then squash fold the
resulting upheaval.

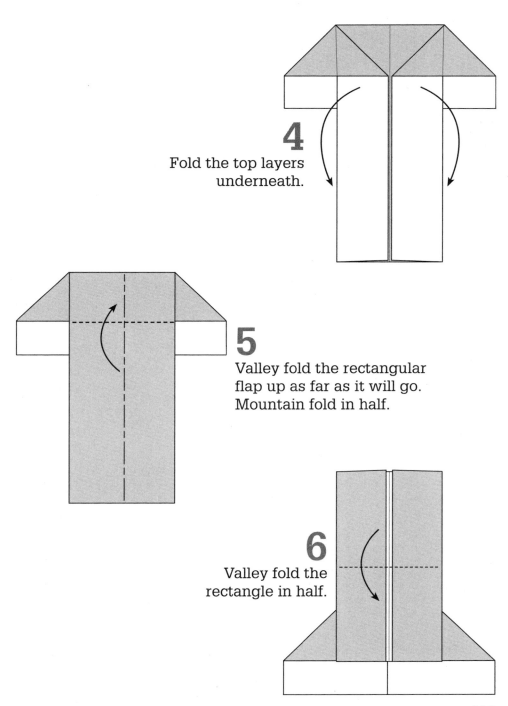

4

Fold the top layers
underneath.

5

Valley fold the rectangular
flap up as far as it will go.
Mountain fold in half.

6

Valley fold the
rectangle in half.

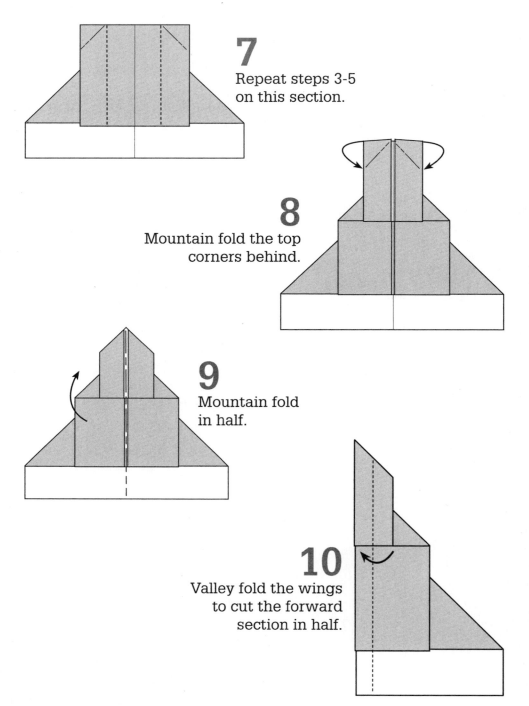

7
Repeat steps 3-5
on this section.

8
Mountain fold the top
corners behind.

9
Mountain fold
in half.

10
Valley fold the wings
to cut the forward
section in half.

11

Valley fold the stabilizers as shown.

12

There are two layers at the front of the main wings. Pull out the innermost layer and squash fold the front to form a third vertical stabilizer.

MULTI-STAGE CRAFT

CORIOLIS MAX

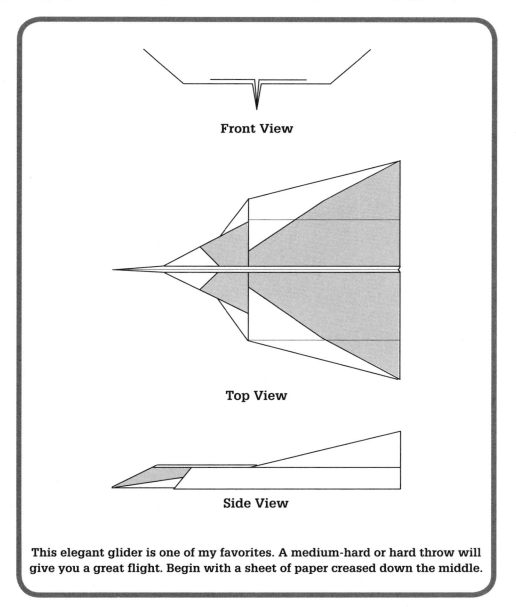

Front View

Top View

Side View

This elegant glider is one of my favorites. A medium-hard or hard throw will give you a great flight. Begin with a sheet of paper creased down the middle.

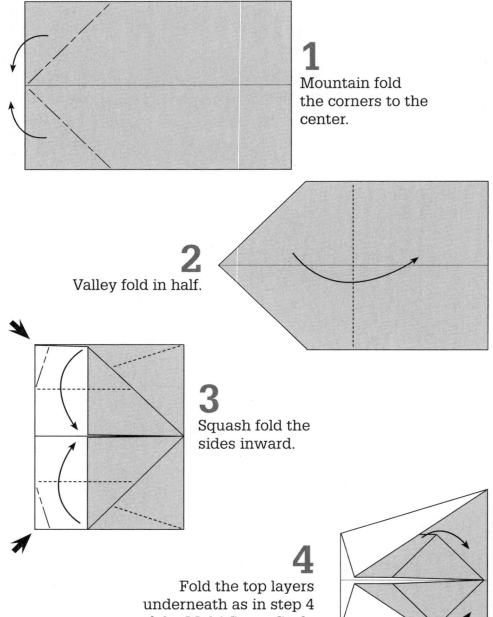

1 Mountain fold the corners to the center.

2 Valley fold in half.

3 Squash fold the sides inward.

4 Fold the top layers underneath as in step 4 of the Multi-Stage Craft.

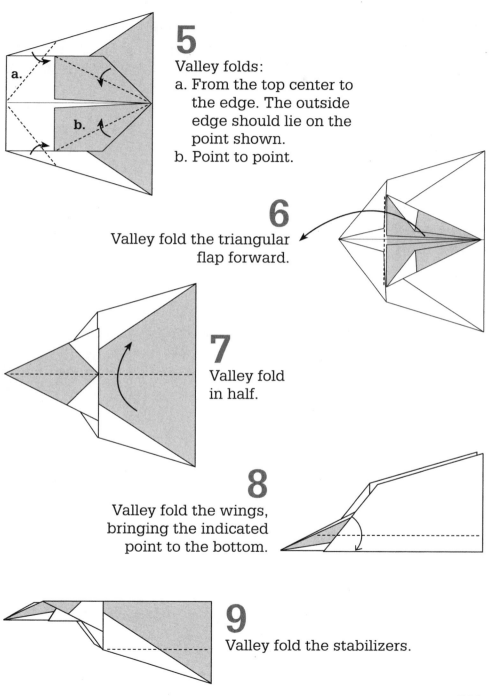

5

Valley folds:
a. From the top center to the edge. The outside edge should lie on the point shown.
b. Point to point.

6

Valley fold the triangular flap forward.

7

Valley fold in half.

8

Valley fold the wings, bringing the indicated point to the bottom.

9

Valley fold the stabilizers.

AEROBOTCH

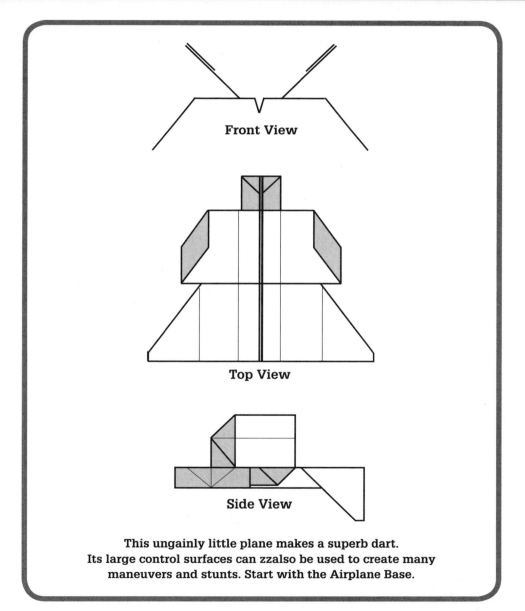

Front View

Top View

Side View

This ungainly little plane makes a superb dart.
Its large control surfaces can zzalso be used to create many
maneuvers and stunts. Start with the Airplane Base.

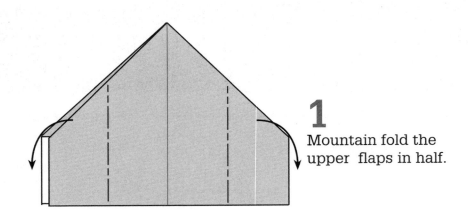

1

Mountain fold the
upper flaps in half.

2

Valley fold in half
again, allowing the
flaps underneath to
flip out.

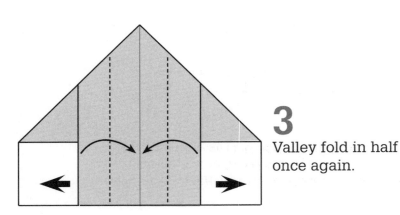

3

Valley fold in half
once again.

4

Now for the fun part: Squash fold the top layer upward following the upper diagonal folds. At the same time you'll have to squash fold a pocket that forms underneath.

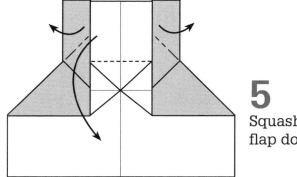

5

Squash fold the upper flap downward.

6

Tuck the two corners underneath the side flaps and sink the top.

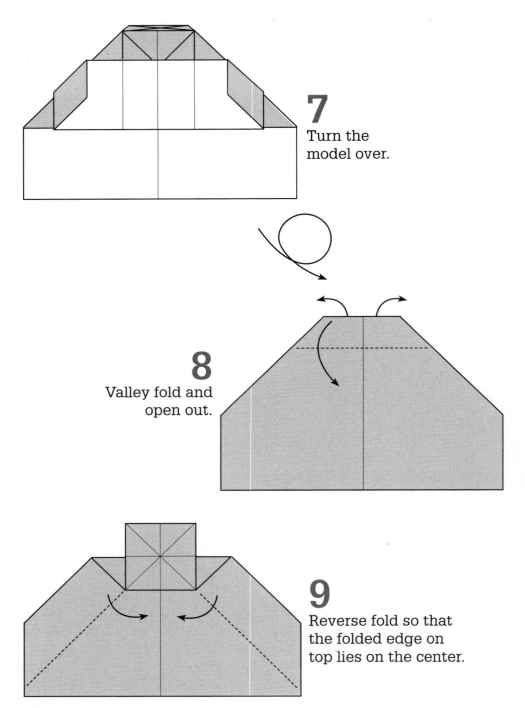

7
Turn the
model over.

8
Valley fold and
open out.

9
Reverse fold so that
the folded edge on
top lies on the center.

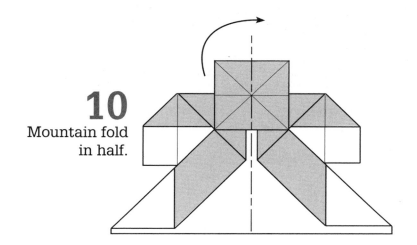

10
Mountain fold
in half.

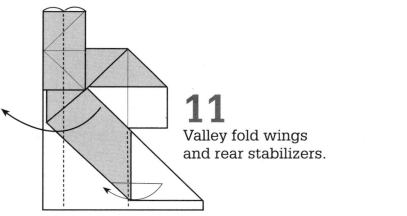

11
Valley fold wings
and rear stabilizers.

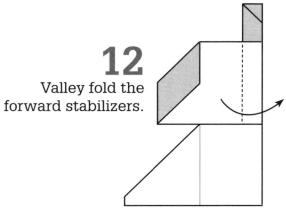

12
Valley fold the
forward stabilizers.

HAMMERHEAD

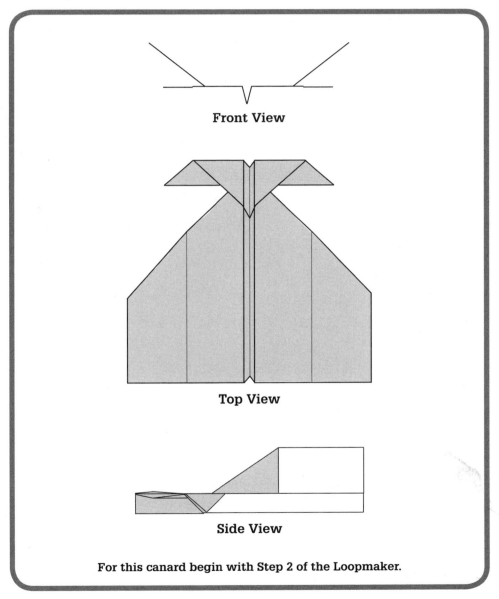

Front View

Top View

Side View

For this canard begin with Step 2 of the Loopmaker.

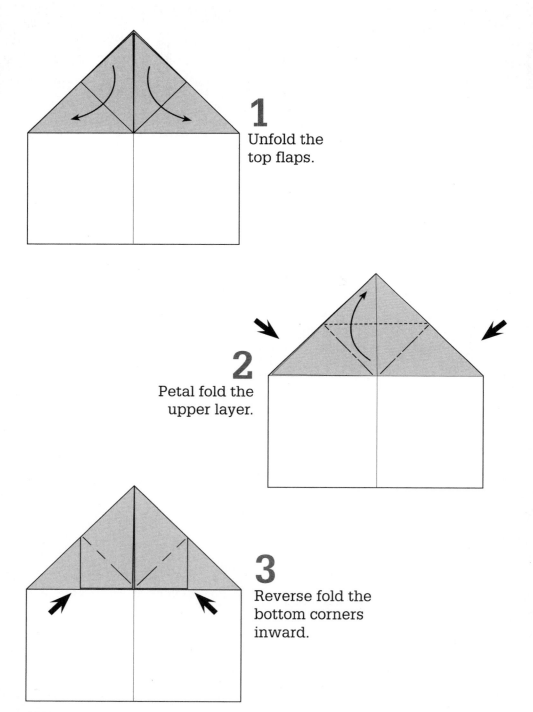

1
Unfold the
top flaps.

2
Petal fold the
upper layer.

3
Reverse fold the
bottom corners
inward.

4

Bisecting the angles at the top, squash fold the upper flaps to the outside.

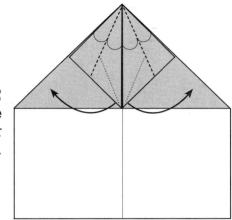

5

There are two points at the top. Mountain fold the lower flap (the one not visible in the drawing) down as far as it will go.

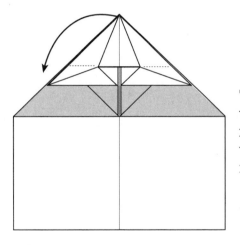

6

Valley fold to form the forward edges of the wings so that the top edge of the wing section (which lies between two layers and is not visible in the diagram) touches the center line.

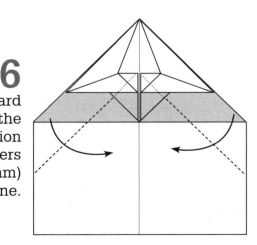

7

Valley fold the
top point down.

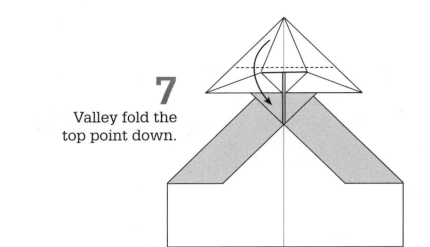

8

Mountain fold
in half.

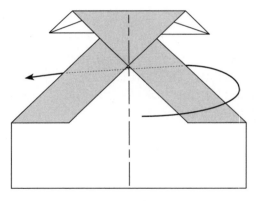

9

Valley fold
the wings.

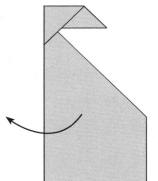

10
Unfold one
side.

11
Mountain fold
the stabilizers.

PAGODOR VOLANT

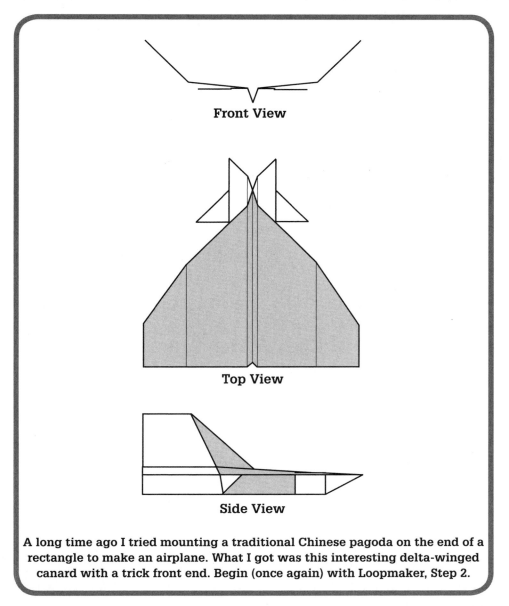

Front View

Top View

Side View

A long time ago I tried mounting a traditional Chinese pagoda on the end of a rectangle to make an airplane. What I got was this interesting delta-winged canard with a trick front end. Begin (once again) with Loopmaker, Step 2.

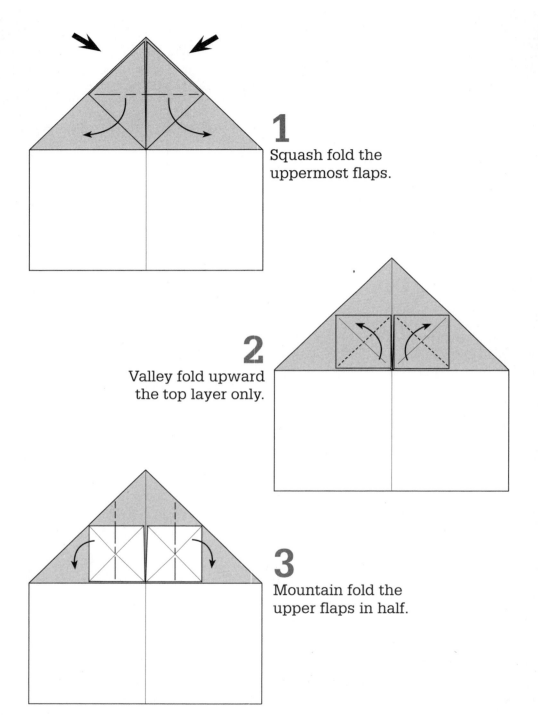

1
Squash fold the
uppermost flaps.

2
Valley fold upward
the top layer only.

3
Mountain fold the
upper flaps in half.

4

Spread the flaps on top apart. This will create a pocket that can be easily flattened.

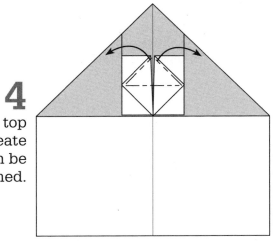

5

Reverse fold both corners inward.

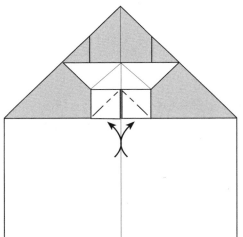

6

Flip so that the point at the top goes behind and the two small triangles flip upward.

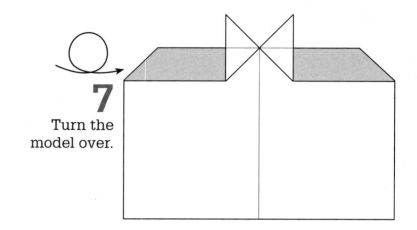

7

Turn the
model over.

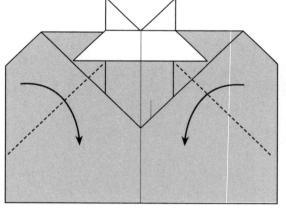

8

Valley fold so the
folded edge on top lies
on the center (this fold
is similar to Step 5 of
the Hammerhead).

9

Mountain fold the
trailing edges of the
wing undersides
behind.

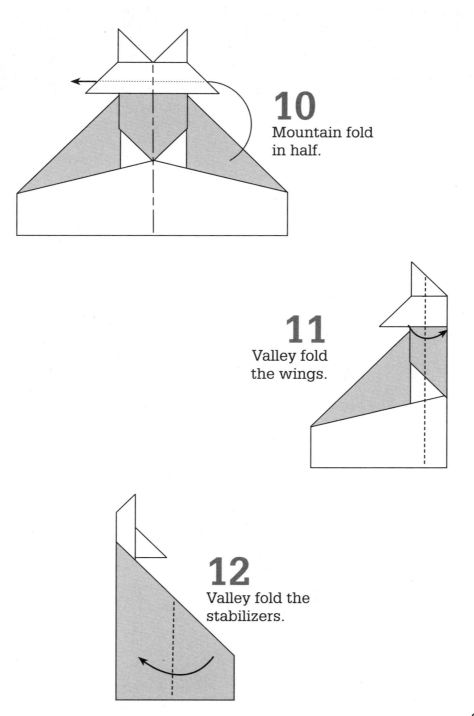

10 Mountain fold in half.

11 Valley fold the wings.

12 Valley fold the stabilizers.

PAGODOR VOLANT

BIPLANE

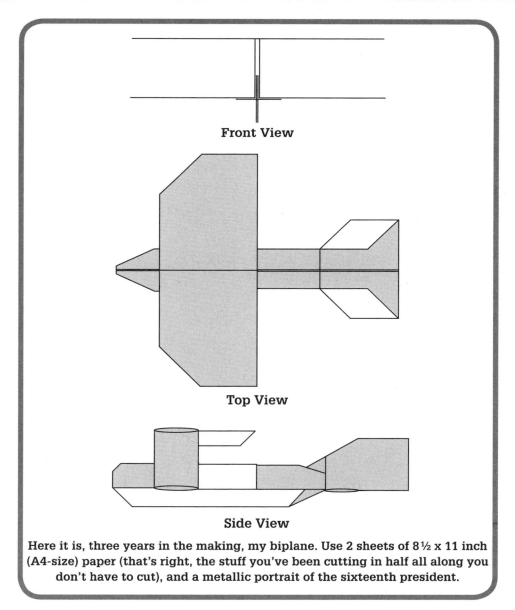

Front View

Top View

Side View

Here it is, three years in the making, my biplane. Use 2 sheets of 8½ x 11 inch (A4-size) paper (that's right, the stuff you've been cutting in half all along you don't have to cut), and a metallic portrait of the sixteenth president.

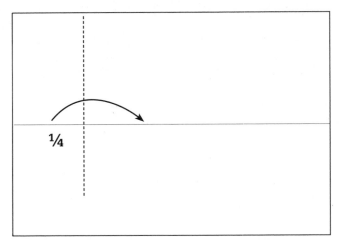

1

Valley fold the paper one quarter of the way in.

¼

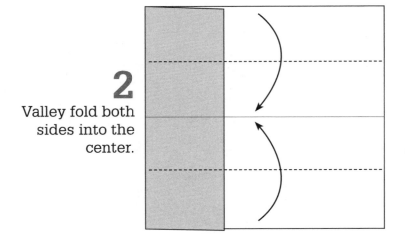

2

Valley fold both sides into the center.

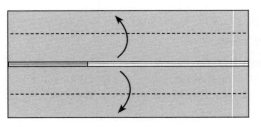

3

Valley fold back out to the edge.

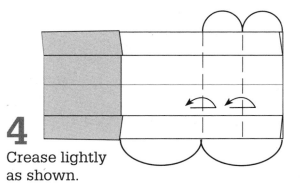

4
Crease lightly
as shown.

5
Valley fold so that the two
creases line up.

6
Pull out and squash
fold the layers hidden
under the top flap.

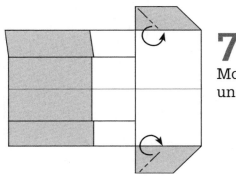

7

Mountain fold the corners underneath, then turn over.

8

Valley fold the long flap over as far as it will go.

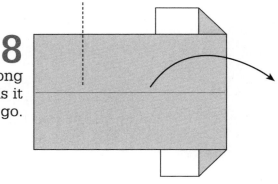

9

Shift the long flap forward.

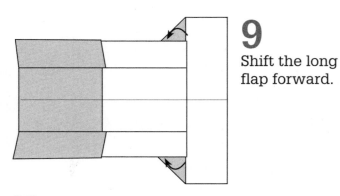

10

Flatten the resulting pockets. No landmarks here, just use your best judgment.

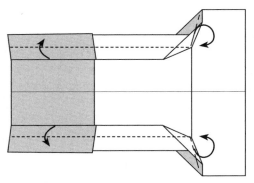

11

Mountain fold the rear of the flap squash folded in the previous step. Valley fold the flaps at the sides in half.

12

Mountain fold the outlying areas behind, then valley fold the model in half.

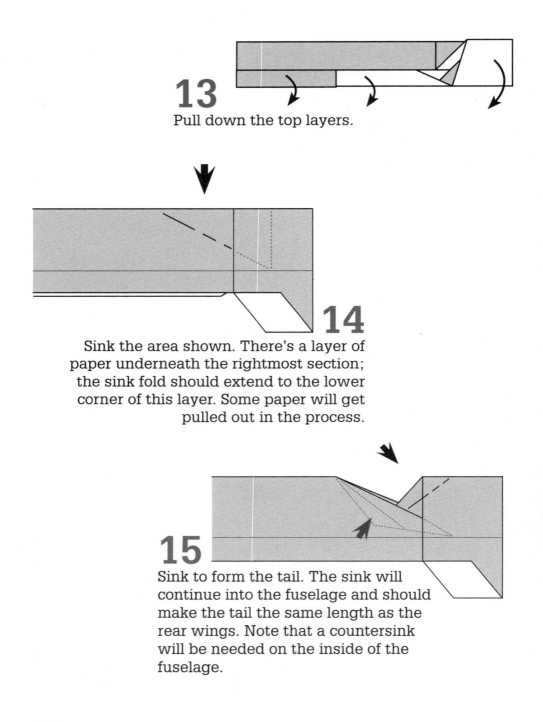

13

Pull down the top layers.

14

Sink the area shown. There's a layer of paper underneath the rightmost section; the sink fold should extend to the lower corner of this layer. Some paper will get pulled out in the process.

15

Sink to form the tail. The sink will continue into the fuselage and should make the tail the same length as the rear wings. Note that a countersink will be needed on the inside of the fuselage.

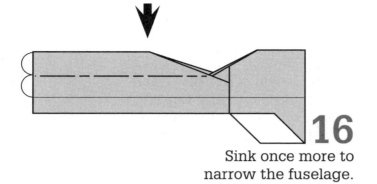

16

Sink once more to
narrow the fuselage.

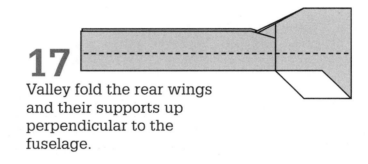

17

Valley fold the rear wings
and their supports up
perpendicular to the
fuselage.

18

Insert a penny into the front.
It should be held in place
between the layer folded in
Step 1 and the rest.

19

The next series of steps is designed to lock the front end together. Start by reverse folding the bottom flap in on one side only.

20

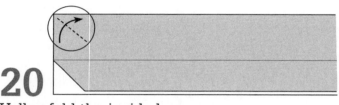

Valley fold the inside layer over to lock the top together.

21

View from the top. Crease the side flap along its angle bisector, then crease into fourths.

22
Reverse fold along the
innermost crease.

23
Part of this is a cutaway view. Roll the
reverse folded flap inside along previously
made creases. Repeat on the other side.

24
Side view again. On the bottom,
tuck the flap from one side into the
pocket created in Step 20. Round off
the top a little with a reverse fold.

Biplane–wings

Another 8½ × 5½ inch (A5-size) sheet of
paper creased down the middle is required.

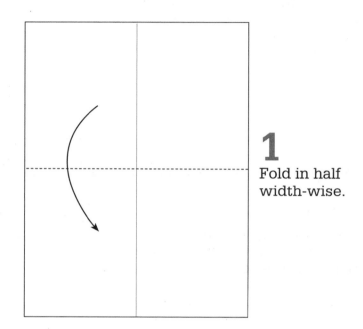

1
Fold in half
width-wise.

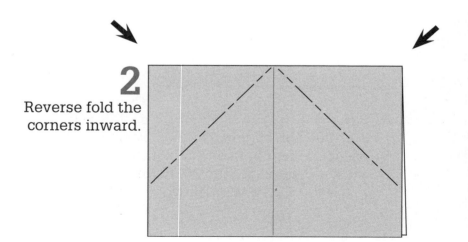

2
Reverse fold the
corners inward.

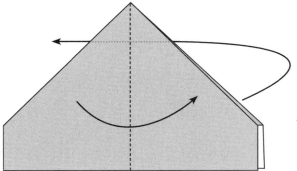

3

Valley fold one flap to the right in front and mountain fold one flap to the left behind.

4

Crease the upper triangle into fourths.

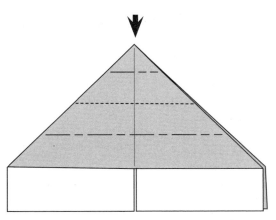

5

Sink up and down.

6

Fit the wings onto the fuselage.

7

Valley fold the lower wings upward along the crease made in Step 17 of the fuselage. Reverse fold the front.

8

Fold the upper wings outward to match the lower wings.

9

Sink the paper left over from Step 8 upward.

10

Squash fold the upper flap so that it lies flat along the wings. Rotate the plane so the top of the wings face you.

11

Sink the two resulting flaps underneath the top layer of the wings. Rotate the model so that its side faces you.

12

Then fold these two flaps down so they rest perpendicular to the wings.

13

Finally, mountain fold the rear portions of these flaps to the center to lock them in place. Fold over a flap inside the front of the wings to lock them together.

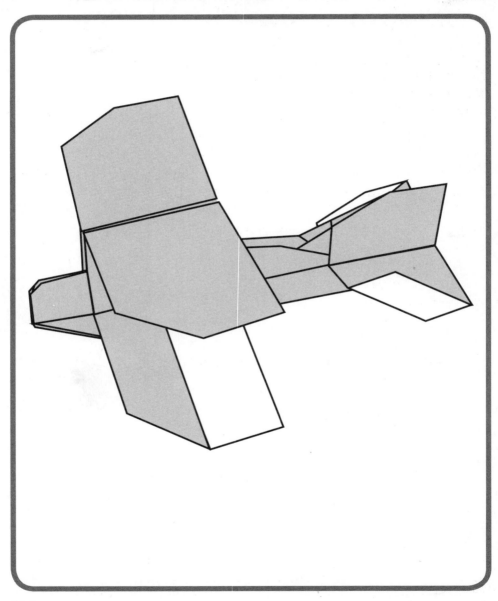